The Stock Administration Book

The Stock Administration Book

Amy Yamashiro, CEP

The National Center for Employee Ownership
Oakland, California

This publication is designed to provide accurate and authoritative information regarding the subject matter covered. It is sold with the understanding that the publisher is not engaged in rendering legal, accounting, or other professional services. If legal advice or other expert assistance is required, the services of a competent professional should be sought.

The Stock Administration Book
Amy Yamashiro

Cover design by Scott Rodrick
Back cover photo credit: Jason Lustig Yamashiro

Copyright © 2005 by Amy Yamashiro.
All rights reserved. No part of this book may be reproduced or transmitted in any form or by any means, electronic or mechanical, including photocopying, recording, or by any information storage and retrieval system, without prior written permission from the author except for the inclusion of brief quotations in a review.

Published by:
The National Center for Employee Ownership
1736 Franklin Street, 8th Floor
Oakland, CA 94612
(510) 208-1300
(510) 272-9510 (fax)
E-mail: nceo@nceo.org
Web: http://www.nceo.org/

ISBN 1-932924-11-6

Contents

Contents v
    Acknowledgements vii
    User's Guide ix

Chapter 1: The Big Picture 1
    Who Are You? 3
    How It Works 4
    Where You Fit In 6
    The Job Itself 8
    How It Gets Done 11
    Stock Administration 12
    Human Resources Coordination 14
    Finance Department Coordination 15
    Resources 16

Chapter 2: Numbers and Formulas 19
    Basic Calculations 20
        Options Outstanding 20
        Shares Authorized for Issuance under the Plan (the Pool) 20
        Shares Outstanding 21
        Shares Granted but Unexercised (Overhang) 21
        Shares Authorized but Unissued 22
        Burn Rate/Run Rate 22
    Basic Reconciliation 23
    Financial Reporting 24
    Accounting Overview 28
        FAS 123 29
        FAS 123(R) 30
        SAB 107 31
        IFRS 2 31
        APB Opinion 25 32
        FIN 28 33
        FIN 44 33
        EITF Issue No. 00-23 34
        FAS 128: Earnings Per Share (EPS) 35

Chapter 3: Plan & Activity Details 37
    Corporate Information 38
    Stock Plan Basics 40
    Nonqualified Compensatory Stock Options (NSOs) 46
    Incentive Stock Options (ISOs) 48
    Restricted Stock Shares (RSS) 54
    Restricted Stock Units (RSUs) 56
    Stock Appreciation Rights (SARs) 58
    Employee Stock Purchase Plan Basics 60
    ESPP Offering Period Specifics 64

    Nonqualified Employee Stock Purchase Plans (ESPPs) 66
    Qualified Employee Stock Purchase Plans (423 Plan ESPPs) 68
    Basic Stock Pool Tracking 74
    Equity Tracking Spreadsheets 76
    Stock Pool Tracking—Summary 77
    Stock Pool Tracking—Detail (1 of 2) 78
    Award Purchase Financing 80
    Stock Tracking (1 of 3) 84
    Shareholder Equity 87
    Equity Activity Checklist 88

Chapter 4: Section 16 91
    Section 16 Filings 92
    Forms 3, 4, and 5 support phone numbers 95
    EDGAR 96
    Section 16 Officer—Initial Information Capture 98
    Section 16 Officer—Stock Holdings 100

Chapter 5: Contacts & Meetings 103
    Equity Compensation Contacts 104
    Stock Administration Team 106
    Calendar 108
    Equity Education 110
    Meeting Details 112

Chapter 6: Regular Updates 115
    Basic Period-End Checklist 116
    Stock Plan Security and Data Retention 117
    Stock Plan Maintenance 118

Chapter 7: Glossapedia 119

Bibliography 201

About the Author 203

About the NCEO and Its Publications 205

Order Form 209

Acknowledgements

It felt like it took forever to finish this book, but it truly would never have gotten done without the many people who helped out in so many ways. Thank you to:

NCEOers Corey Rosen, Scott Rodrick, Luke James, Sam Shah, Matthew Lea, Colleen Kearney, Deborah Krant, Eimear Elzy, Richard Cuthrell, Pat Boykin, and Pam Chernoff for their support through the gestation of first a baby then a book.

Chris Yamashiro and Linda Lustig for so much help in so many ways, not the least of which has been providing endless grandma playtime, meals, and other help, often with little or no notice.

All of my family and friends for unceasing encouragement and support.

Special appreciation and gratitude goes to the following industry experts who generously gave of their time and energy to review and improve this book:

Barbara Baksa, CEP, Executive Director of the National Association of Stock Plan Professionals, provided an extremely thorough review and detailed comments on the first draft of this book. It would not be nearly as accurate or complete as it is now if not for her.

Emily Cervino, CEP, of the Certified Equity Professional Institute; Michelle Murcia, CEP.

Pam Van Gordon, CEP, Vice President, Advisory Services, of Stock & Option Solutions, Inc., gave a careful review with "big picture" insight, which completely changed the tone of this book for the better.

Dan Walter, CEP, fortunately chose to apply his great breadth and depth of knowledge to a very exacting review, providing conscientious feedback and a much more accurate book.

And there's no way this book would ever have happened if not for my amazing husband Jason Lustig Yamashiro. His indefatigable encouragement, incredible patience, and thoughtful insights never cease to astound me.

Amy Yamashiro
El Cerrito, CA

For Kalen and Alton Yamashiro,
who have given up more "mommy time" than they'd like so that this book could be written.

User's Guide

Every time I've told an in-house stock administrator about this book, the immediate response has been something like: "Wow, I wish I'd had that when I started!" Which is exactly why I wrote this book.

My first experience with equity compensation was when I became the executive assistant (EA) to the CEO at a startup company. I began by following instructions left for me by the previous EA, but it became clear pretty quickly that things had been done neither accurately nor correctly for some time. As the phone bill for legal services rose, so did my understanding of how things should have been done and what I needed to do to fix them. We realized that a complete overhaul of numbers and records was needed—a situation I would come to realize was fairly standard for a startup. I enjoyed the challenge so much that I switched over to contracting to concentrate solely on the company's stock administration and was fortunate enough to be able to take that company through its IPO (early 2000—what a time!).

Being able to take a company through so many different phases of growth helped me realize why this is such a fantastic field—it's brand new! There's always something new to learn and anything can be improved. The only down side is that this emerging field doesn't have a whole lot of training built in.

This book is your practical training guide: a handbook to get you through the day. Obviously, though, there is a lot more to stock administration than can possibly be covered in this short book. This is not designed to answer every question that will arise as you go about doing your work. It is meant to be an introduction to the basics, help you navigate the day-to-day questions you may encounter, give you an overview of salient points about less common situations, or to be used as a efficiency aid and quick reference guide by those already in the field.

SECTION ONE: Chapter 1: The Big Picture

Especially if you're new to the field, take a few minutes to step back and look at the big picture. Once you've got a good feel for who, what, and how, the website links provided as resources are a "must-read."

As much as the rest of this book delves into the technical points or details on what to do and how to do it, you need to start off by knowing why and how you're there. It's fine to be able to do your job function as presented, but for greater impact on the organization, take time to understand how you fit into the corporate machinery and where you can make a difference.

SECTION TWO: Chapters 2–6: Templates and Basic Knowledge Blocks

This section contains templates for immediate use, data collection forms, and some quick reference points. Don't worry about trying to go through in order, just jump around as needed. The templates or data collection pieces are italicized in the table of contents for ease of use.

All of the templates are accompanied by step-by-step instructions to make completion as easy as possible, which can make the page breaks a little funny. The CD attached to the back cover has printable/usable versions of the templates. You can complete the forms electronically, print out multiple blank copies, or just photocopy the forms from the book. Do whatever works best for you.

Remember—these documents are designed to be fairly universal, so you will probably want to track additional information or in a modified format. Go ahead! These are working documents, so change them to be what you need.

And the basic knowledge blocks are just that—basic. Just as cliff notes give you the information but complete texts let you experience all the nuances and subtleties, assume that there's more to know than is presented here, but this is a good first step.

SECTION THREE: Chapter 7: Glossapedia
This section is something that started out to be a glossary, but took on a life of its own and is now more than a glossary, but less than an encyclopedia . . . a "glossa-pedia!"

I realized that when I look something up in a glossary, it usually tells me just enough that I can then go look it up somewhere else to find the more extensive information I was looking for. You may find that this does the same thing for you, but it's at least a little more comprehensive than most.

As a general rule, you should assume that the issue discussed is far more complex than presented, but now at least you have some basic information so that you can research it further. For more detailed information about any of the topics covered, or to seek information about something you don't see mentioned here, please consult either primary sources or your company's legal counsel. The web links provided as Resources in Chapter 1 should take you pretty far, as will the book list provided as a bibliography.

International Issues
It is *very* important to note that there is a calculated lack of information about the handling of international issues in this handbook. There are so many issues unique to each country and situation that it is impractical to even attempt to cover them in this format, so instead of spotty coverage, there's none. Never assume that international treatment will be the same as in the U.S. The best advice I can provide is for you to find and work closely with local counsel and human resources experts to accomplish your goals in each country.

Comments and Suggestions
If you have amazing documents of your own that you'd like to share, make changes you feel others would want to know about, or just want to pass along suggestions or comments, please send them on over to *amy.yamashiro@gmail.com* for inclusion in a future version of this book. Thanks for using this book!

Chapter 1: The Big Picture

Who Are You?

Let's start with you and work out from there. As a person with responsibility for handling equity distribution at your company, you might be called a stock administrator, comptroller, equity specialist, executive assistant, general counsel, stock plans manager, or any of a number of other titles. You may be a Certified Equity Professional or you may not know what a plain vanilla stock option is. You may work in finance, legal, human resource, administration, or be a department unto yourself.

Unlike a position such as "investor relations" or "salesperson" there is no clearly designated space on a boilerplate organizational chart for you. That is one of the beautiful challenges of this profession. You are in the forefront of a new discipline, helping shape a field of expertise that didn't exist 30 years ago. Think Webmaster. Think IT. What will stock administration as a standard corporate function look like in ten years?

There was a time when equity was tracked by hand on paper. Then the new technology became computer spreadsheets. Now there are equity tracking software programs designed to not only hold your data but to produce a whole range of reports for you with the simple input of parameters or variables as well.

Similarly, stock administration in most companies started out as a plan established and managed by legal counsel, handled in house as a small piece of an executive assistant's broad job function. For many private companies, it still sits there. Now, though, with the myriad new reporting requirements imposed by recent legislation, it would be an odd public company or large private company that didn't have multiple people with responsibility for different aspects of company equity.

Currently, stock administration is defined as a cross-departmental function, requiring current knowledge and expertise in areas of accounting, taxation, human resources, law, and securities regulation. It demands not only the ability to work with a variety of different people outside the company (vendors, brokers, transfer agents, consultants, etc.), but the capability to coordinate with multiple departments within the company (IT, finance, human resources, legal, compliance, etc.). It also includes being the public face of the company to anyone holding or working with company equity, especially communications to employees, optionees, and shareholders needing to know how equity issues affect them.

Do you recognize yourself anywhere in this?

How It Works

Now that we know who you are, the question becomes: "How does it all happen?"

In the very beginning, someone has a grand idea for a product or service and decides to start a company. The company is established and incorporated, and the corporation is approved to issue a certain number of shares of certain classes of stock. Founders and initial investors purchase stock. Now a stock plan is drafted and approved by the board of directors and shareholders and a certain "pool" of shares is reserved for issuance under the plan.

An equity award starts its life cycle with a request for approval or ratification by the board of directors. Since the mechanics of stock options, stock appreciation rights, and restricted stock all work in basically the same way (and stock awards essentially just skip to the exercise of a fully vested award), we'll use a stock option for this example. Once approved, the option is granted to the optionee and that number of shares becomes "outstanding" and is removed from the stock option pool. The optionee receives a notice of grant, a copy of the grant agreement, a form of notice of exercise, and a copy of the plan document, of which certain pieces must be signed and returned to the company for filing. The company agent, usually the president or CEO, countersigns and the grant is active until the optionee's separation of service from the company or the expiration date of the award, whichever comes first.

If the optionee terminates service, any unvested options are canceled, and there is a specified period of time in which the vested options can be exercised, after which the optioned shares will be canceled as well. If service continues but the optionee wishes to exercise an option, most plans allow for the exercise of tranches of options as desired, with no change in any other aspects of the option grant. Some plans allow for the exercise of unvested options, in which case the stock received will be restricted until fully vested. If an unvested option is exercised, the optionee should consider filing a Section 83(b) Election for tax purposes.

An option is exercised by the delivery of both a signed notice of exercise and payment for the shares being exercised to the company. The exercise might be processed in-house or by a brokerage with a certificate for the shares printed in-house, recorded on the books of the company, delivered to a brokerage account, or physically delivered by a transfer agent. The shareholder's tax holding period for capital gains purposes begins when the option is exercised. If the shares are exercised in a same-day sale, where the exercise is paid for by the sale of some of the purchased shares, the long-term capital gains tax rate is not available and any taxes owed are calculated at the short-term capital gains tax rate. Once the option has been exercised, the optionee receives shares and becomes a shareholder of the company.

The shares held may freely tradable or they might be restricted securities, either unregistered under the Securities Act of 1933 or owned by a control person or affiliate and subject to Rule 144 holding periods. Any restrictions on share transferability will be explained by the legend(s) printed on the reverse of the "legended" share certificate.

This new shareholder now receives annual reports on the financial and operating status of the company, as well as access to any other information necessary to make informed voting decisions annually either at the annual shareholders' meeting or by proxy.

To become a public company, the company must make an initial public offering of shares, occurring after a rigorous examination of corporate records and documents called "due diligence" provides the information necessary for the company to file registration statements with the SEC. Once the securities of the company are registered for sale, a significant portion of the equity in the company is brought to the trading market for purchase and sale by the public.

Public companies are subject to reporting requirements under Section 12 of the Securities Exchange Act of 1934, which necessitate the filing of 10-K (annual) and 10-Q (quarterly) reports, among other things. In addition, certain officers and directors of the company are subject to reporting requirements under Section 16 of the Securities Exchange Act, requiring the filing of Forms 3, 4, and 5. All SEC filings can and should be done electronically via EDGAR, the SEC's electronic data gathering, analysis, and retrieval system.

Your company may be at any point along this path from inception to publicly traded company. But what part do you play in all this?

Where You Fit In

Now we get to see the equity award life cycle from your perspective.

Let's say you've been with the company since inception, handling the equity piece—and fortunately, you know exactly what you're doing. When the company was founded and shares first purchased, you started a spreadsheet to track shareholder equity positions and a binder containing all board and shareholder actions pertaining to each class of equity.

When the stock option plan was created, you filed copies of the board and shareholder approvals with all exhibits in a binder for the plan. When the board next met, you prepared a list of proposed option grants for approval that contained the full name of each award recipient, the number of shares to be granted, the date of vesting commencement, and the date of grant (which for any employees receiving ISOs but not yet hired will be the date of hire). After the board meeting, you confirmed the approval of the option grants and filed a copy of the board minutes in your binder. You then started a spreadsheet to track option activity under this plan, with a corresponding summary by approval date.

You prepared grant notices for each optionee and filed the notice run in your binder behind the minutes approving the grants. You assembled packets containing two copies of the notice of grant, a grant agreement, a notice of exercise, and a plan document, then distributed the grant packets with instructions for the optionee to sign and return both notices of grant. You collected all of the grant notices and had the company agent (usually the President) countersign them, and returned one original to the optionee. You then filed the original grant notices in files by optionee, noting the presence of a signed original on the board approval list in your binder or on your spreadsheet.

To make sure you hold all the current information on new hires, terminations, option grant approvals, and other internal equity transactions, you maintain a good working relationship with clear communication and data flow paths between stock tracking, human resources, the person preparing the board packets, and the person holding the approved minutes.

In a report from human resources you see a terminated employee holding vested options. You cancel the unvested options as of the date of termination and prepare a letter to the terminated employee containing information on the number of options vested and available to exercise, the exercise price and amount, a notice of exercise, the option expiration date, and instructions on the exercise process. The employee soon comes to you with a notice of exercise and payment by check; you make three copies of both. You process the transaction and print a record of the transaction which includes monies paid and taxes withheld, print out the certificate, making sure to print the appropriate legends on the reverse, and make three copies each of these. The original check goes to accounting/payroll by the end of the day with a copy of the notice and transaction record, the original certificate with a copy of the check, the notice, and the transaction record goes to the employee, the original notice and transaction record with a copy of the check and, the certificate go in the employee file, a copy of each will go in your stock option exercise binder, and a copy of the certificate goes in your stock register binder.

You regularly provide reports to finance on the equity holdings of the company, and provide any information needed for reports they produce as well as for regular audits. You begin holding regular employee information panels about your stock option plan. You hold regular trainings to ensure that hiring managers understand the plan and the language they can use with prospective employees. You implement an equity tracking software program to replace your spreadsheets.

And then the company decides to go public. All of a sudden there's a flurry of demands for information and clean data. Auditors appear to be living at your offices. You receive numerous requests for copies of documents and to have your records examined. You have most of your office photocopied and delivered to attorneys. The data you provide is examined, reorganized, recategorized, and rechecked for accuracy. You handle a lot of exercise activity and have to update your reports daily. You find out that "the printer" isn't the same thing as a graphic design firm or a mailing house and that the streets are really empty after midnight on weekdays. You bring in outside experts to explain stock ownership, tax implications, and brokerage interactions to your employees. And finally, you go live and your stock is available for trading on the public market.

Now that your company is publicly traded, you file Form 3s for all your Section 16 officers. You develop and maintain relationships with a captive broker and a transfer agent. Data is transferred regularly between both and you're responsible for making sure it's all completely accurate. You keep copies of blanket opinions on hand to fax to outside brokers handling legended stock certificates. You resolve innumerous issues around employees, stock options, and brokers. You maintain regular communication with all your Section 16 officers to ensure prompt filing of all Form 4s. And you still need to keep up with all the grant and exercise activity, maintaining communications with HR on employee status and updating information quickly enough to send accurate files to the broker and transfer agent.

There's so much to do that you decide to either hire more people or outsource your stock administration. You start looking into firms and services. You start itemizing your company's needs. Then you realize that to figure out what you want to end up with, you need to know where you're coming from. In other words, just what is it you do, anyway?

The Job Itself

Just what exactly do you do? That's a tough question to answer. You can be as broad as the job description posted by your company, you can define your work as a pattern of interactions and data flows, or you can dive right into the nitty-gritty details of your daily schedule. Here we look at the broad job description.

Just for fun, go through this basic list of job functions, responsibilities, and skills to see how many of these pieces you hold, help with, or possess. Double credit if you can insert "international" or "global" in the item as well.

Overview Function
- Keep current with equity compensation related legislation, regulations, and practices.
- Monitor, improve, and adapt processes for efficiency and to accommodate new changes and requirements.
- Management, administration, coordination, reporting, and reconciliation of all equity compensation programs
- Offer input and make recommendations based on knowledge of industry standards, competitive landscape, benchmarking data and service methodologies and models.
- Act as company liaison, coordinating and monitoring information flow and communications, between vendors, brokers, transfer agents, internal departments, employees, optionees, and shareholders.

Administrative Activity
- Develop and maintain processes involved in the granting, exercise, and cancellation of equity grants such as stock options, restricted stock and other related vehicles.
- Design, plan and implement stock programs
- Monitor share balances/reserves.
- Establish and maintain stock plan database
- Maintain corporate records for the stock plans
- Maintain and update employee equity intranet site
- Day-to-day management and administration
    - Grant processing—prepare and distribute grant agreements
    - Record keeping—paper and electronic filing and storage systems
    - Exercise processing—coordinate with broker, transfer agent
    - Terminations/cancellation processing—coordinate with human resources
    - Dividend processing—calculate and distribute
- Coordination with internal departments, providing regular reporting on tax, payroll, accounting, and human resources interactions
- Audits and reconciliation reports preparation
- Periodic plan statement to participants
- Coordination with transfer agents and brokers

Executives/Directors
- Prepare and audit equity compensation award lists and reports for Board meetings.
- Maintain processes to ensure officer and director compliance with insider trading and other related policies and regulatory requirements such as Section 16.
- Administer executive/director compensation plan, including bonus or incentive plans and deferred compensation.
- Manage executive/director retirement payments.

Compliance
- Work with consultants, auditors, record keepers, vendors, and trustees to help assure compliance with all rules and regulations pertaining to equity compensation plans.
- Maintain processes to ensure equity plans are in compliance with SEC, NYSE, NASDAQ, and/or other SRO governance policies.
- Maintain processes to ensure option grants are in compliance with the stock plans and limits established by the Board of Directors and Compensation Committee.
- Maintain processes to ensure employee compliance with insider trading and stock ownership policies, including blackout windows.
- Maintain processes to ensure officer and director compliance with Section 16, including preparing required SEC filings.
- Maintain processes to ensure stock administration compliance with Sarbanes-Oxley 404.

Reporting
- Run annual/quarterly/monthly/weekly reports as needed.
- Prepare information and reports regarding executive and director compensation for inclusion in annual report.
- Prepare, coordinate, audit, and reconcile reports for required SEC filings: includes Section 16, 10-K, 10-Q, proxy statement, any registration statements such as Form S-3 or S-8.
- Prepare, coordinate, audit, and reconcile information and reports for SRO (NYSE, NASDAQ, etc.) filings.
- Prepare, coordinate, audit, and reconcile information and reports for FAS 123 calculations, option usage, overhang, and other financial reports as needed.
- Prepare, coordinate, audit, and reconcile stock income and tax withholding reports with payroll.
- Reconcile monthly reports on common shares outstanding and plan balances with transfer agent.
- Prepare quarterly and fiscal year forecasts for basic and diluted shares.

Communication
- Prepare, update, and distribute equity plan materials.
- Answer employee questions and resolve problems regarding equity plans.
- Facilitate employee communications and education about equity programs, including questions or issues with the company's broker or transfer agent.
- Educate hiring managers on language and terminology around equity compensation.
- Facilitate regular communications between stock brokers, transfer agents, and human resources department for administering stock plan activity.
- Annual Meeting preparation and coordination.
- Communicate stockholder information and/or changes to employees.

Relationships
- Be accessible to employees across all levels and business cultures.
- Support and interact with Legal, Treasury, Finance, and Payroll regarding proxy reporting, 8K filings, 10K filings, 10Q filings, Sarbanes-Oxley 404 compliance, etc.
- Support and interact with Human Resources to process equity compensation pieces of employee hires and terminations.
- Maintain positive relationships with the captive broker and transfer agent; cooperatively monitor share and plan balances/reserves, resolve any stock related issues.
- Manage outsourced administrators to handle daily equity administration matters including data integrity, equity grants, and terminations/cancellations.
- Negotiate commissions with brokers.

Basic Skills
- Certified Equity Professional
- Knowledge of stock option & restricted stock regulations.
- Attention to detail
- Strong written and oral communication skills.
- Strong writing, speaking, and presentation skills.
- Strong analytical and problem solving skills
- Strong time management skills
- Strong accounting and analytical skills
- Strong organizational skills
- Proficiency in numerous software programs, both office and equity tracking
- Self-motivated
- Ability to multi-task in a fast-paced environment
- Ability to make decisions on complex tasks and problems with minimal supervision
- High level of confidentiality
- Demonstrated initiative and good judgment in resolving issues
- Strong customer service ethic
- Strong interpersonal skills to manage interactions between multiple departments
- Ability to work well and establish confidence and credibility with executives, senior professionals, directors, and investors.
- Expertise in project management
- Expertise in financial analysis, statistical analyses and spreadsheet modeling
- Membership in NASPP, NCEO, or GEO

Other
- Assist with M&A activities; integration of company plans on acquisition.
- Train, supervise, and manage team members.
- Additional duties as assigned.

Next we'll more carefully define how you do what you do.

How It Gets Done

Now you can start to piece together that pattern of interactions and data flows. Look at all these pieces and think through how each activity progresses from start to finish. Who is involved and in what capacity?

Some people might call this "documenting processes." As you know, section 404 of the Sarbanes-Oxley Act of 2002 requires annual management reports on internal controls and procedures for financial reporting—which includes stock administration. Check to see what you already have in place. In many cases, company policy is to have a very basic procedural process outlined as your official compliance piece. In that case, don't call this "procedural process" but "in case I drop dead and someone else has to come in and take up where I left off without my input." Be sure to think of it that way as you're writing.

Another thing to think about as you go through this is how important accuracy is at each step. What checks and balances do you have in place to be sure things are done right? Has everything that can be automated been automated?

And any chain is only as strong as its weakest link. Especially in your interactions with other departments and outside vendors, picture the worst case scenario then figure out what you could have done to prevent it.

This is a great place to identify areas that can be improved upon, as well as critical areas that need backup plans in place. Try to make time on a regular basis to review and update; for example, as part of your year-end checklist, when there's a change in staffing on your team, or just before you go on vacation. Remember, an ounce of prevention is worth a pound of cure!

These pieces are broken out over the next few pages into three general areas of departmental involvement: Stock Administration, Human Resources, and Finance.

Stock Administration

- **Grant Approval Process**

    Do you have a grant approval process? What is it? Who determines who will receive grants and how much will be granted? Who prepares the report for approval? Do you act on board or committee approval? After the grants are approved, how is that information passed along to you? How is the grant information (recipient, plan, type, term, vesting, number of shares, option price) verified? What is the timeframe for approval of grants? How is the grant price/fair market value determined? Who ensures compliance with ISO limitations, ESPP limitations, and plan limits and provisions?

- **Grant Tracking**

    What is your procedure for grant tracking? How and where do you file grant approvals? Board minutes documenting grant approvals? Hardcopies of grants? Electronic copies? Sent vs. signed and returned grants? Do you track grants through a stock administration program in-house in addition to outsourcing? How is the grant information (recipient, plan, type, term, vesting, number of shares, option price) verified?

- **Grant Distribution**

    How do you distribute equity grants? By hand/interoffice mail/postal service/express mail/e-mail/intranet/Web access? Are grant agreements printed on paper or sent electronically? Are they produced in-house or do you outsource your grant distribution ? What is the timeframe from approval of grants to distribution? How is the grant information (recipient, plan, type, term, vesting, number of shares, option price) verified? Do you require the recipient to sign and return the grant or do you have a negative response policy? Is there a timeline/deadline for signing and returning grants?

- **Equity Status Inquiries**

    Where do your grantees go to find out the status of their equity compensation? Do you handle requests in-house or do you outsource? Do you make the information available by Web access/phone/e-mail?

- **Exercising Equity**

    What is your procedure for the exercise of grants? Do you allow the exercise of unvested stock? Do you process exercises in-house or do you outsource your exercises? How do you confirm exercisability of options? List any legends placed on the backs of your certificates and to whom they apply. How do you track exercises? Do you send a confirmation of exercise from the company at the time of exercise? Who generates the report? Who sends it? Who is responsible for Section 6039 compliance?

- **Stock Sales**

    Does the shareholder need to contact the company for any reason before selling stock? Attach a copy of any/all blanket opinions you have. Do you have a right of first refusal attached to any stock? What are your pre-sale compliance requirements? How do you track disqualifying dispositions?

- **Equity Status Reporting**
  Who generates regular equity status reports? How often are they generated/sent? Who sends them? How are they sent? Do you keep paper or electronic copies? Where? Do you send notices of impending grant expiration? How often? How many months prior to expiration do you send the report? Who generates the report? What do you include in the notification? Who sends it?

- **Shareholder Tracking**
  Who is responsible for maintaining a shareholder listing? Is this outsourced or do you track in-house? Who tracks common stock? Preferred stock? Warrants? Restricted stock? What is the company policy on abandoned property? Who handles the escheatment process?

- **Compliance**
  Who is responsible for making sure your company meets all compliance requirements? Who files Forms 3, 4, and 5? If the person with primary responsibility is out of the office, who are the next two people in line and do they know what their responsibilities are in terms of knowing when they assume responsibility? Who files 10-Q and 10-K reports? Who handles legended/restricted stock sales? Does your company allow 10-b(5) plans and if so, how are they handled? Who sends notice of blackout periods? By what method?

- **Annual Shareholders' Meeting**
  When is your annual meeting held? What is the date of record? Who is responsible for creation of the shareholder listing at the date of record? What is quorum for shareholder approval? Who prepares the proxy statement? Who sends it? Who tallies votes?

- **Shareholder Communications**
  Who is responsible for shareholder communications? How often are shareholder communications sent? What is typically sent, a letter/brochure/packet? Where are copies of all communications and attachments stored?

- **Definitions and Interpretations**
  Who provides interpretations of terms or plan documents when questions arise? In what way are situational definitions documented? How do past events affect future decisions? Include all lists of definitions and/or glossaries associated with your equity compensation arrangements.

- **Data Retention**
  Who is responsible for data organization and storage? Hardcopy? Electronic? Where is each piece of data maintained? For how long is each piece of information retained?

- **Data Security and Recovery**
  List all persons with access to each set of records maintained: for each stock plan, who is involved? To what extent do outsource providers or external vendors have access to confidential information? Who authorizes access? Who monitors access privileges? Who is responsible for compliance with data privacy laws? How often is electronic information backed up? Do you have a disaster recovery plan?

Human Resources Coordination

☐ **Participant Tracking**
How do you track optionee/employee/shareholder information? If in a database, how often are changes entered? By whom? From whom do you receive information to be tracked and how is the change authorized? If new hire information comes from HR, do changes in contact information also come from HR or directly from the contact? How are the changes recorded? When address changes are made, what controls are in place to ensure compliance with applicable interstate or international tax issues?

☐ **Recruitment**
Create a document to give to all hiring managers that explains the type(s) of equity compensation your company offers as well as the specific information they can discuss with candidates. Be very clear about what they can and can not discuss. Describe the grant process so that they will know that they cannot guarantee options will be granted at a certain price or on a given date.

☐ **New Hire Information**
Each new hire should receive the same information as every other new hire about each plan they will participate in. Prepare distribution packets for each plan, along with a checklist for each plan of documents that should be given out as well as returned. Will you give the new hire his or her individual grant information at the same time? Include an acknowledgement of receipt of documents for signature and return.

☐ **Leaves of Absence/Changes in Status**
How are leaves of absence handled? Who is involved? How does the information get to you? How are leaves of absence documented? Is award vesting suspended for the duration of the leave of absence? Do you send notification of imminent loss of ISO status?

☐ **Termination of Employment**
When an employee is terminated or a service contract involving equity comes to an end, how are you notified? Do you receive a regular report on terminations from HR? Who generates the report and is responsible for it getting to you? Is that report sent to an outsource company or do you enter it into your stock administration program? Who verifies the accuracy of termination information and cancellation of grants?

Finance Department Coordination

- **Equity Accounting**

    Who decides what type and how much equity will be granted? Who is responsible for making the assumptions used in fair value pricing? Who records amounts recognized as the result of equity grants? How is it tracked? Who coordinates the collection of information for 10-Q and 10-K reports? Proxy materials? Investor materials? Shareholder materials? What equity information is provided at the annual meeting?

- **Payroll Items**

    On what schedule are payroll runs made? Do you have a system for transmitting includible amounts to payroll? Do you transmit exercise information to payroll on a daily basis to cover next day deposit situations? Do you have a payroll deduction component to any of your stock plans? How does it run? Who manages it? When NSOs are exercised, do you withhold for taxes by check or in stock? Who tracks amounts to be included on W-2 or 1099 forms? At year-end, when do you give W-2/1099 figures to Payroll?

- **Exercising Equity**

    Do you process exercises in-house or do you outsource your exercises? How do you verify exercise costs and payment receipts? How do you track exercises? Have you assigned the following tasks to allow for separation of duties and adequate second-person auditing: payment collection, processing deposits, general ledger entries, processing exercises, and dispersing checks/shares?

- **Sale of Stock**

    Does your company retain repurchase rights? How do you track disqualifying dispositions?

- **Backdated Transactions**

    What is your procedure for dealing with information that either needs to be entered after the fact or changed on the books? Who needs to be included in this process? What changes are made to the approval process? How is the information recorded and the changes registered? Who makes the changes, approves the changes, and verifies their accuracy?

- **Reconciliations**

    Do you perform reconciliations of: common stock outstanding, preferred/other stock outstanding, option/SAR/restricted shares outstanding, shares authorized for issuance, shares authorized but unissued, capitalization tables, and all transaction totals? If not, who does? What other items do you reconcile? How often? Monthly? Quarterly? Annually?

Whew! With all that, can anyone really be expected to do it all alone? Beyond your team and corporate structure, where can you turn for help?

Resources

Fortunately, in this internet age, a wealth of information is readily available. Some of the best resources available are primary sources and industry organizations.

Government Agencies and Regulatory Bodies
Financial Accounting Standards Board (FASB): http://www.fasb.org/
International Accounting Standards Board (IASB): http://www.iasb.org/
Internal Revenue Service (IRS): http://www.irs.ustreas.gov/
    Withholding rates: http://www.irs.gov/publications/p15/index.html
    Internal Revenue Code (U.S. Code, Title 26, Government Printing Office version):
        http://www.gpoaccess.gov/ecfr/index.html
    Internal Revenue Code (U.S. Code, Title 26, Office of the Law Revision Counsel version):
        http://uscode.house.gov/
Securities and Exchange Commission (SEC): http://www.sec.gov/
    EDGAR: http://www.sec.gov/edgar.shtml
    SIC codes: http://www.sec.gov/info/edgar/siccodes.htm
    Section 16 forms: http://www.sec.gov/about/forms/secforms.htm#EDGAR
    Securities Regulations online: www.law.uc.edu/CCL/xyz/sldtoc.html
U.S. Department of Labor (DOL): http://www.dol.gov/
U.S. Department of the Treasury: http://www.ustreas.gov/
    Foreign exchange rates: http://www.federalreserve.gov/releases/h10/update/
    Historical exchange rates: http://www.federalreserve.gov/releases/h10/hist/
    Treasury bond interest rates: http://www.federalreserve.gov/releases/h15/data.htm

Certification Agency
Certified Equity Professional Institute (CEPI): http://cepi.scu.edu/

Equity-Related Organizations
Beyster Institute: http://www.beysterinstitute.org/
Global Equity Organization (GEO): http://www.globalequity.org/
National Association of Stock Plan Professionals (NASPP): http://www.naspp.com/
National Center for Employee Ownership (NCEO): http://www.nceo.org/
Society for Human Resource Management (SHRM): http://www.shrm.org/
WorldatWork: http://www.worldatwork.org/

Information Resources
Fairmark Press: http://www.fairmark.com/
Frederic W. Cook & Co., Inc.: http://www.fwcook.com/
Institutional Shareholder Services (ISS): http://www.issproxy.com/;
ISS news service: http://slw.issproxy.com/
MyCriticalCapital: http://mycriticalcapital.com/
MyStockOptions.com: http://www.mystockoptions.com/
Romeo & Dye's Section16.net: http://www.section16.net/
Steve Huddart's option value calculator: http://www.smeal.psu.edu/faculty/huddart/
Stock-Options.com: http://stock-options.com/
TheCorporateCounsel.net: http://www.thecorporatecounsel.net/

Stock Exchanges and Trading Systems
American Stock Exchange: http://www.amex.com/
	Holidays and Hours: menu item "At the Amex" – "About Amex" – "Holiday Calendar"
NASD: http://www.nasd.com/
NASDAQ: http://www.NASDAQ.com/
	Holidays and Hours: http://www.nasdaq.com/about/schedule.stm
New York Stock Exchange (NYSE): http://www.nyse.com/
	Holidays and Hours:
	http://www.nyse.com/Frameset.html?displayPage=/about/1022963613686.html
Pink Sheets: http://www.pinksheets.com/

IRS Forms & Publications
1040: http://www.irs.gov/pub/irs-pdf/f1040.pdf
1040 instructions: http://www.irs.gov/pub/irs-pdf/i1040.pdf
1099-B (gross transaction proceeds): http://www.irs.gov/pub/irs-pdf/f1099b03.pdf
1099-B instructions: http://www.irs.gov/pub/irs-pdf/i1099b.pdf
1099-MISC (taxable income): http://www.irs.gov/pub/irs-pdf/f1099msc.pdf
1099-MISC instructions: http://www.irs.gov/pub/irs-pdf/i1099msc.pdf
5500: http://www.irs.gov/pub/irs-pdf/f5500.pdf
5500 instructions: http://www.irs.gov/pub/irs-pdf/i5500.pdf
6251 (AMT): http://www.irs.gov/pub/irs-fill/f6251.pdf
6251 instructions: http://www.irs.gov/pub/irs-pdf/i6251.pdf
SCH C: http://www.irs.gov/pub/irs-pdf/f5500sc.pdf
SCH C instructions: http://www.irs.gov/pub/irs-pdf/i1040sc.pdf
Publication 525 "Taxable and Nontaxable Income": http://www.irs.gov/pub/irs-pdf/p525.pdf
W-2 (taxable income): http://www.irs.gov/pub/irs-pdf/fw2.pdf
W-2 instructions: http://www.irs.gov/pub/irs-pdf/iw2w3.pdf
W-7: http://www.irs.gov/pub/irs-fill/fw7.pdf
W-8BEN: http://www.irs.gov/pub/irs-pdf/iw8ben.pdf

And don't forget that there's a glossapedia at the end of this book. Between here and there, though, are those nitty-gritty details we mentioned earlier.

Chapter 2: Numbers and Formulas

It doesn't matter if you started life as a "numbers person" or not, working with numbers accurately and efficiently is a big part of what you do. Let's face it, stock administration is a financial reporting function—it's all about the numbers. If the numbers are accurate, you're doing your job. If the numbers are off, just what is it you've been doing?

You will be asked for certain figures on a regular basis, and you need to know how to get them. That said, if you've never worked with these before, make sure you double- and triple-check your figures and calculations with someone who has, to be sure you have a complete understanding of how they work, before providing them to others. Some plans have unusual quirks or features that reach beyond the scope of the very basic information provided here.

"Basic Calculations" walks you through calculations for *Options Outstanding, Shares Authorized for Issuance, Shares Authorized but Unissued, Shares Outstanding, Overhang,* and *Burn Rate,* then *"Basic Reconciliations"* walks you through the mechanics of a very simple reconciliation using those formulas. And *"Financial Reporting"* is a checklist version of a working form to assemble some of the basic information needed to produce any one of a number of financial reports.

"Accounting Overview" is a reference section that gives you a very brief look at only the key points of the accounting standards and methods most relevant to your work, touching on pieces of APB Opinion 25, FIN 44, EITF 00-23, FAS 123, FAS 123R, IFRS 2, and FAS 128 (EPS). Please be aware that many areas of FAS 123R were still in the process of being clarified at the time this book went to press; check for more current information before relying solely on the information provided herein.

Basic Calculations

Options Outstanding
(a + b – c – d = e)

Any plan starts with zero options outstanding. Options granted become outstanding. Options exercised or canceled cease to be outstanding.

a) + Beginning options outstanding _____
    The number of options outstanding at the end of the last reporting period

b) + Options granted _____
    The number of options granted in this reporting period

c) – Options exercised _____
    The number of options exercised in this reporting period

d) – Options canceled _____
    The number of options canceled (forfeited, expired, etc.) in this reporting period

e) = Ending options outstanding _____
    The number of options outstanding at the end of this reporting period

Shares Authorized for Issuance under the Plan (the Pool)
(a – b + c + d + e = f)

Any stock plan states the number of shares authorized for issuance under the plan, often called the "pool." Grants decrease the number of shares available to issue. Canceled grants are usually returned to the pool to be available again, depending on the terms of the plan. Repurchased shares often do not return to pool, so are not included in this calculation. Returned shares include those approved for grant but not issued, shares exercised but withheld to pay taxes, or SARs paid in cash so that the reserved shares are no longer restricted. Any time the number of shares available for issuance is increased by shareholder/board approval or due to evergreen additions, adjust the pool to include the new shares.

a) + Shares authorized _____
    The number of shares initially authorized for issuance under the plan.

b) – Shares/options granted _____
    The number of shares/options granted.

c) + Shares/options canceled _____
    The number of options canceled (includes forfeited, expired, etc.).

d) + Shares/options returned _____
    The number of shares withheld for taxes, reserved or granted but unissued.

e) + Shares added _____
    The number of shares added by shareholder vote or by evergreen provisions.

f) = Current shares authorized for issuance _____

Shares Outstanding
(a + b + c + d + e + f − g − h = i)

Any company, have it one plan or eight, has a specified number of shares authorized for issuance, beginning with the number of shares issued in the initial public offering (IPO). Options exercised for stock, phantom stock or SARs exercised for shares, restricted shares, restricted stock units, ESPP shares, and subsequent offerings all increase the number of shares outstanding. Shares repurchased and/or canceled by the company decrease the number of shares outstanding.

- a) + Beginning shares outstanding _____
    The number of shares outstanding at the end of the last period/reconciliation
- b) + Options exercised _____
    The number of options exercised during this reporting period
- c) + SARs _____
    The number of shares issued on exercise of SARs
- d) + Restricted shares _____
    The number of restricted stock shares issued
- e) + ESPP shares _____
    The number of ESPP shares issued
- f) + Stock Issues or Offerings _____
    The number of shares added by other issues of stock or subsequent offerings
- g) − Shares repurchased _____
    The number of shares repurchased by the company
- h) − Shares canceled _____
    The number of shares canceled by the company
- i) = Ending shares outstanding _____
    The current number of shares outstanding

Shares Granted but Unexercised (Overhang)
((a + b) / c)

This is one basic formula for calculating overhang, the number of options with potential to convert into shares and dilute ownership percentages. The exact formula used differs from firm to firm doing the calculation, but no one standard formula is in widespread use. See the Glossapedia for more common overhang formulas.

- a) + shares outstanding _____
- b) + shares available _____
- c) ÷ total shares outstanding _____

Shares Authorized but Unissued
(a + b = c) *or* (a − b + c = d)
This number combines the calculations you've already made above—Options Outstanding and Shares Authorized for Issuance.

    a) + Shares Authorized for Issuance _____

    b) + Options Outstanding_____

    c) = Shares Authorized but Unissued _____

Or use the other form of this calculation to double check your figures from above.

    a) + Shares authorized _____
          The number of shares initially authorized for issuance under the plan.

    b) − Options exercised_____
          The number of options exercised in this reporting period

    c) + Shares/options returned _____
          The number of shares withheld for taxes, reserved or granted but unissued.

    d) = Shares Authorized but Unissued _____

Burn Rate/Run Rate
(a / b)

The rate at which a company issues equity compensation. ISS basically recommends that the average three-year burn rate be no more than two percent of the common shares outstanding. See "Burn Rate" in the Glossapedia for more detail.

    a) + equity awards granted annually _____

    b) ÷ common shares outstanding _____

Basic Reconciliation

1. Plan/Item _____
2. Reconciliation date _____
3. Reconciliation period _____

	a. date	b. amount
4. As of <last period end>	_____	_____
5. <adjustment date & amount>	_____	_____
6. As of <current period start>	_____	_____

7. Basic Calculation (see previous pages)

8. As of <current period end>	_____	_____

N.B. When performing a reconciliation, you should always refer back to your source documents for figures rather than to your work papers. This ensures that any errors made in calculation are not repeated throughout the process. That said, also attach any work papers providing figures that will be used going forward.

1. What is being reconciled? Basic figures that should be reconciled at least monthly include stock outstanding, options outstanding, shares authorized for issuance, and shares authorized but unissued.
2. On what date is this reconciliation being made?
3. What period does this reconciliation cover?
4. a) On what date did the last period end?
   b) What was the amount at the end of the last period (amounts may be in shares or dollars)?
5. a) On what date(s) did any adjustment(s) take place? Add lines as needed for transactions that took place after the last period closed and attach documentation—once a period closes, any adjustments with dates in the closed period must appear as adjustments to an open period.
   b) What was the amount of the adjustment?
6. a) On what date did the current period start?
   b) This number should equal 4.b + 5.b (+ 5.b , etc.) or 4.b with no adjustments.
7. Perform the basic calculation for the item you are reconciling.
8. a) On what date did the current period end?
   b) This is the number you will use on any or all other reports asking for this figure!

Financial Reporting

1. Is this for a 10K, a 10Q, or some other report?
2. Date on which the reporting period began.
3. Date on which the reporting period ended.
4. Date on which the figures for report are being prepared.
5. The person to whom this information will go.
6. The date by which this information should be given to the person above.

Data: checkmark then complete the items needed for the report being prepared, realizing that the name of the report your software program provides may be different from that used here but should contain the information described.

7. Prepare and attach a narrative description of each plan identified, including the number of shares authorized for grant of options or other equity instruments, and general terms of awards under the plan such as vesting requirements, and maximum term of options granted.
8. To find the stock closing price on last trading day of the period, go to www.nasdaq.com , click on the Charts tab, enter your company's trading symbol in the box, click GO, then click anywhere on the 1-year pricing chart to get a list of daily closing prices for the past year.
9. If the CEO is not in the top five, include the CEO report as well. These reports should include: Summary Compensation Table (value of restricted stock grants, number of stock option grants, number of SAR grants, long term incentive plan (LTIP) payouts), Option/SAR Grants in the Last Fiscal Year (number of securities granted, percentage of total grants that year, exercise price, expiration date, potential realizable value), Aggregate Option/SAR Exercises in the Last Fiscal Year (shares acquired on exercise, value realized, number of exercisable unexercised options/SARs, number of unexercisable unexercised options/SARs, value of unexercised options/SARs), and LTIP Awards in the Last Fiscal Year (number of shares/units/rights received, vesting period, estimated future payouts).
10. $(a + b - c - d = e)$
    a) The number of options outstanding at the end of the last reporting period
    b) The number of options granted during this reporting period
    c) The number of options exercised during this reporting period
    d) The number of options canceled, forfeited, or expired during this reporting period
    e) The number of options outstanding at the end of this reporting period
11. The same calculation as above, but broken out by option exercise price. Most stock tracking systems can provide you with this report.
12. The same calculation as above, but only the exercisable options. If possible, have your stock tracking system provide you with this number.

Financial Reporting

1. 10K/10Q/ _____
2. Reporting period start date _____
3. Reporting period end date _____
4. As of _____
5. Provide to _____
6. By no later than _____

Data

7. ☐ Summary of Equity Compensation Plan(s) _____
8. ☐ Stock closing price on last trading day of period _____
9. ☐ Equity positions of the five most highly compensated executive officers. Attached: Y/N
10. ☐ Options Outstanding (a + b − c − d = e)
    a. + Beginning options outstanding _____
    b. + Options granted _____
    c. − Options exercised _____
    d. − Options canceled, forfeited, expired _____
    e. = Ending options outstanding _____
11. ☐ Options Outstanding by Price Range. Attached: Y/N
12. ☐ Options Outstanding and Exercisable by Price Range. Attached: Y/N

Financial Reporting

13. For #10, the vesting going forward. If possible, run from your stock tracking program.
14. For each piece of this item, you may enter a value for this period and a value for the same period in the last reporting year.
    What model do you use to value your options? Black-Scholes or another method?
    a. Stock option exercise price.
    b. Fair market value of the underlying stock on the grant date.
    c. Expected option life—explain how you arrived at this assumption. The expected life of an option should be at least equal to its vesting period, with the company's historical exercise data taken into account.
    d. Does your company distribute dividends? If not, this = 0. If so, calculate the yield based on the expected life from above.
    e. Average risk-free interest rates for Treasury bonds with the same term as the expected option life (above), that were issued during the current period. To get this, go to www.federalreserve.gov/releases/h15/data.htm – Treasury constant maturities. If there are no Treasury bonds with terms equal to the expected option term, take the average of the two Treasury bond terms that most closely approximate the expected option term.
    f. Volatility—explain how you arrived at this assumption, using either your own company's data or (if permitted) similar industry index data.
15. Using the variables above, what is the average weighted fair value for this reporting period? Your stock tracking program should be able to provide this number.
16. What was the fair value for the same reporting period in the last reporting year?
17. Using the variables above, what is the fair value for this year-to-date? Your stock tracking program should be able to provide you with this number.
18. Value forfeited options for the current reporting period.
19. What compensation expense will you record for this reporting period for options?
20. What compensation expense did you record for options for the same reporting period last year?
21. What compensation expense will you record for options for this year-to-date?
22. What compensation expense will you record for this reporting period for all stock-based equity compensation?
23. What compensation expense did you record for all stock-based equity compensation for the same reporting period last year?
24. What compensation expense will you record for all stock-based equity compensation for this year-to-date?
25. Provide the terms of any significant modifications made to stock-based equity compensation during this period.

Financial Reporting

13. ☐ Vesting schedule of options outstanding at end of period. Attached: Y/N
14.   current period   same period last year

    ☐ Valuation Method: Black-Scholes / _____   B-S / _____

       a) ☐ Exercise price _____ _____

       b) ☐ Market price of underlying stock _____ _____

       c) ☐ Expected life of options _____ _____

       d) ☐ Dividend yield _____ _____

       e) ☐ Risk-free interest rate _____ _____

       f) ☐ Volatility _____ _____

15. ☐ Fair Value: current period _____
16. ☐ Fair Value: same period in last reporting year _____
17. ☐ Fair Value: year-to-date _____
18. ☐ Valuation of forfeited options _____
19. ☐ Compensation Expense—Options: current period _____
20. ☐ Compensation Expense—Options: same period in last reporting year _____
21. ☐ Compensation Expense—Options: year-to-date _____
22. ☐ Compensation Expense—All: current period _____
23. ☐ Compensation Expense—All: same period in last reporting year _____
24. ☐ Compensation Expense—All: year-to-date _____
25. ☐ Award Modifications. Attached: Y/N

Accounting Overview

Until 2006, there are two different accounting standards in use—APB 25 and FAS 123—which can sometimes cause confusion as the same activity can be accounted for in very different ways at different companies. If an employer corporation chooses to account for equity compensation under APB 25, which provides very favorable accounting treatment by permitting stock options to be accounted for using the intrinsic value method, it is required to disclose on a pro forma basis in the footnotes to its income statement what its earnings and earnings per share would have been under FAS 123. FAS 123, however, which requires fair value accounting for stock options, is the standard preferred by the Financial Accounting Standards Board (FASB), which in December 2002 offered alternative transition methods and disclosure provisions in an attempt to facilitate an expected movement toward FAS 123 adoption.

When the International Accounting Standards Board (IASB) moved forward in 2001 to create a new accounting standard for equity compensation, FASB was impelled to follow suit, issuing an Exposure Draft in March 2004 followed by a final standard in December 2004: FAS 123R "Share-Based Payment." A revision of FAS 123 "Accounting for Stock-Based Compensation," FAS 123R supersedes and eliminates the alternate use of intrinsic-value-based accounting under APB Opinion 25.

FAS 123R becomes effective:

- For public entities that do not file as small business issuers—as of the beginning of the first interim or annual reporting period that begins after June 15, 2005

- For public entities that file as small business issuers—as of the beginning of the first annual reporting period that begins after December 15, 2005

- For nonpublic entities—as of the beginning of the first annual reporting period that begins after December 15, 2005.

Until FAS 123R becomes effective, however, APB 25 and FAS 123 remain in effect as originally issued. The following is a very brief overview of some of the most salient points of each of the pieces of guidance currently providing oversight to accounting for equity compensation.

FAS 123/FAS 123R/IFRS 2

FAS 123
"Accounting for Stock-Based Compensation," released in October 1995; replaced by FAS 123R in December 2004.

Mandatory for transactions with nonemployees exchanging goods or services for equity instruments; optional for transactions with employees. Applies to transactions in which an entity receives goods or services and pays for them with either equity instruments or cash in an amount linked to the value of its equity instruments.

Allows companies to continue to account for stock options under APB 25 if the required note to financial statements that describes their stock options discloses the pro forma impact that accounting for these stock options under the fair value approach of FAS 123 would have on net income and earnings per share.

- Requires that the fair value of an option be estimated at grant using an option pricing model (Black-Scholes or binomial model) with subsequent modifications based on:
- Risk of forfeiture reflected by not recording expense for forfeited options.
- Restrictions on transferability of vested options reflected by estimating option values based on the expected life of the option rather than on its full contractual life.
- Requires that option pricing models consider six factors in determining an option's fair value:

    (1) exercise price;

    (2) current market price of underlying stock;

    (3) expected life of the option;

    (4) expected dividends on the underlying stock;

    (5) expected interest rate on risk-free securities during the expected life of the option; and

    (6) expected volatility of underlying stock (generally not applicable for nonpublic companies).

- States that the "fair value" concept can be expressed as a basic formula: (option fair value) = (intrinsic value) + (time value-money) + (time value-volatility). The intrinsic value, or spread, is the advantage of holding an option rather than buying the underlying stock directly. The time value-money is the value of money not spent on the exercise price but invested somewhere else. The time value-volatility is the profit from stock appreciation without a risk of loss; the higher the volatility, the larger the opportunity to gain.
- States that when fair value cannot be reasonably estimated (for example, if the option has a floating exercise price or the stock has a floating conversion ratio), the initial measurement is at the current intrinsic value. It is then updated as factors change, with fair value measured as soon as an estimation is feasible.
- Sets a narrower safe harbor for noncompensatory plans than under APB 25, so many plans deemed noncompensatory under APB 25 are compensatory under FAS 123. For

instance, an ESPP can allow only a 5% discount with no look-back to be noncompensatory under FAS 123.

- Requires employers to provide descriptions of their stock-based compensation plans, including the general terms of awards, as well as further disclosures.
- Recognizes no difference between fixed and variable plans.

FAS 123(R)

"Share-Based Payment" is a revision of FAS 123 "Accounting for Stock-Based Compensation," issued December 2004; supersedes and eliminates the alternate use of intrinsic-value-based accounting under APB Opinion 25. FAS 123, as originally issued, is effective until FAS 123(R) becomes effective.

Applies to transactions with employees or nonemployee directors; does not affect transactions with nonemployees (refer to SAB 107 for effects). Does not affect tax-qualified ESOP activity. Applies to transactions in which equity instruments of any kind are used as compensation for goods or services, primarily employee services.

Public entities must measure fair value of equity instruments at grant date, recognized over the service period, with no compensation cost recognized for forfeited awards. Fair value for liability awards is measured at each reporting date until settlement, with any change in value recognized over the affected service period.

- Options and awards subject to cliff vesting accrue expense on a straight-line basis over the vesting period ("single grant life"); expense for options and awards with graded vesting may be recorded on either a straight-line basis over the full service period or in an accelerated manner where each vesting increment is treated as a separate award ("multiple grant life").

- Nonpublic entities may choose between measuring fair value of liability awards at grant date or intrinsic value at each reporting date until settlement. Historical volatility of an industry sector index may be substituted for expected volatility.

- Compensation cost is recognized over the service period, generally presumed to be the vesting period, and no compensation cost is recognized for forfeited awards.

- Fair value is estimated using Black-Scholes or other similar option-pricing models allowing for variable inputs unless observable market prices for the same or similar instruments are available.

- Equity award modifications resulting in higher fair value measurements result in incremental compensation costs.

- Allows nondiscriminatory ESPPs with a maximum 5% discount and no look-back or similar features to qualify for the noncompensatory exemption.
- Requires recognition of deferred tax assets based on grant date fair value of awards (refer to FAS 109 for details).
- Provides stock-settled SARs with essentially the same accounting treatment as stock options.

- Is in substantial convergence with the IASB final standard on Share-Based Payment (IFRS 2), except for transactions with nonemployees and private companies, and with small differences with regard to modifications, liabilities, and income taxes.

SAB 107

Issued by the Securities and Exchange Commission staff, Staff Accounting Bulletin 107 provides guidance to help with the implementation of FAS 123R. Includes interpretive guidance with regard to transactions with nonemployees, transition from nonpublic to public company status, valuation methods, accounting for certain redeemable financial instruments issued under share-based payment arrangements, classification of compensation expense, non-GAAP financial measures, modification of options prior to adoption of FAS 123R, and disclosures in MD&A subsequent to adoption of FAS 123R.

- Requires recognition of nonemployee equity transactions based on the more reliably measurable fair value of either the good or service received or the equity instrument issued.
- Suggests that the guidance in FAS 123R be applied by analogy to areas that are not specifically addressed in other authoritative literature to produce generally relevant and reliable financial statement information.

IFRS 2

International Financial Reporting Standard 2 "Share-Based Payment," released by the International Accounting Standards Board in 2004. In substantial convergence with FAS 123R: only significant areas of difference are described below.

- Requires modified grant date method for share-based payment arrangements with nonemployees rather than measurement at the earlier of either the date on which the recipient commits to performance requirements or the date on which the performance goals have been reached.

- Further restricts the noncompensatory exemption for ESPPs.

- Does not differentiate between public and nonpublic entities beyond allowing nonpublic entities to substitute historical volatility of an appropriate industry sector index for the expected volatility.

- In tax jurisdictions such as the U.S., where the time value of stock options is generally not tax deductible, does not allow the recognition of deferred tax assets for the compensation cost related to the time value component of the fair value of an award. Allows recognition of deferred tax assets only if and when the options have intrinsic value that might be tax deductible. In contrast, FAS 123R requires recognition of deferred tax assets based on grant date fair value of an award.

APB Opinion 25

Accounting Principles Board Opinion No. 25, issued in 1972; superseded by FAS 123R; will be completely phased out for all companies by the end of 2006.

Applies only to equity instruments granted to employees; accounting for equity instruments granted to nonemployees falls under FAS 123.

- **Measurement cost**: the "intrinsic value" of options, meaning any "spread" or amount by which the FMV exceeds the exercise price.
- No compensation cost is recognized if stock is issued through noncompensatory plans, defined as those where:
    - Only employer stock may be issued.
    - Substantially all full-time employees meeting limited employment qualifications may participate.
    - Options and awards are granted equally or based on a uniform percentage of salary (the number of shares an employee may purchase may be limited).
    - The discount from the market price at the date of grant is no greater than the discount reasonable in an offer to stockholders or others. A 15% discount is a safe harbor.
    - If the plan is in the form of options, the time permitted for exercise is limited to a reasonable period—27 months is safe harbor, up to 5 years is permitted for options with strike price not set until date of exercise.
- Plans with look-back options can qualify as noncompensatory plans (section 423 plans are an example).
- Requires the employer to expense the compensatory value of options in its financial statements on the basis of two key principles:
    - The compensatory value of stock options consists only of the spread.
    - This compensatory value is measured as of a measurement date that is the first date on which both the number of shares optioned and the option exercise price are known.
- Compensation expense should be charged to expense over the periods expected to be benefited. If it's not clear whether options are for current or future services, companies should presume that they are for service in the period in which they are granted or awarded, or in prior periods. When the service period is not clear, it should be presumed to be the vesting period.
- **Variable plans**: For all non-option plans and for option plans whose terms are or can be varied (such as the expiration date, price, or vesting conditions), compensation is measured as the amount by which the FMV of the shares of the corporation's stock covered by the grant exceeds the option price or value specified. Changes in the FMV of those shares between the date of grant and date of measurement result in a change in the measure of compensation for the right or award, generally by "marking to market" the increase or decrease in the current intrinsic value of the award (the amount that, if fully vested and exercised, would be realized). This amount is adjusted to reflect vesting.

- **Fixed plans**: Compensation cost, if any, on a fixed award should be recognized using a systematic and rational method over the total service period (generally on a straight-line basis).

FIN 28

FASB Interpretation No. 28, "Accounting for Stock Appreciation Rights and Other Variable Stock Option or Award Plans" issued December 1978. Provides interpretation of APB Opinions 15 and 25.

- Compensation expense for SARs and other variable awards should be measured at the end of each period as the amount by which the FMV of the underlying stock exceeds the option price or value specified by the plan and should be recorded over the service period.
- Changes to the FMV result in adjustments to accrued compensation and compensation expense in the periods in which the changes occur until the date on which both the number of shares and purchase price, if any, are known.

FIN 44

FASB Interpretation No. 44, "Accounting for Certain Transactions Involving Stock Compensation, an Interpretation of APB Opinion No. 25," issued March 2000. Provides additional guidance and clarification to issues raised under APB 25.

- Options granted to consultants are not covered by APB 25 and are thus valued under FAS 123, but remeasured each quarter.
- A change in status from employee to consultant will result in a compensation charge with respect to the unvested portion of outstanding options as if a new grant had been made on the date of the status change.
- Modifications to previously fixed options, including: option cancellations or reissuances, option term extensions or renewals, and addition of accelerated vesting to existing grants if the grants would otherwise have been forfeited, will generally result in a new measurement date, producing expense based on the intrinsic value added by the modification.
- Modifications to previously fixed options, including: change in exercise price, change in the number of shares being optioned, addition of reload feature, and repricing (cancellation and reissue within a six month period is also considered repricing) will result in variable accounting from the modification date through the exercise date.
- If the terms of the plan specify that tax withholding with stock may not exceed the statutory federal and state minimums, and the optionee has no discretion to determine the amount of withholding, such withholding will not result in variable accounting at exercise.
- Options that include "cash bonus" features, including payment contingent upon exercise or unfixed bonus amounts, will result in variable accounting.

EITF Issue No. 00-23
Emerging Issues Task Force Issue No. 00-23, "Issues Related to the Accounting for Stock Compensation under APB Opinion No. 25 and FASB Interpretation No. 44," issued 2000; provides further guidance and clarification of issues raised by APB 25 and FIN 44.

- 6+1 option repricing: Cancellation of options followed by replacement six months and one day after cancellation results in variable accounting if the replacement formula is connected in any way to stock fluctuations during the 6+1 period.
- Adding transferability to an otherwise fixed option will not result in variable accounting unless it is determined that the transferability is for the purpose of either employer reacquisition or accounting rules circumvention.

FAS 128: Earnings Per Share (EPS)

FAS 128 requires that entities present on the face of their income statements: (1) basic EPS for income from continuing operations and for net income; (2) diluted EPS for income from continuing operations and for net income (unless there are no dilutive instruments issued, meaning only common stock is outstanding).

Basic EPS is computed by dividing reported earnings available to common stockholders by weighted average shares outstanding.

- Shares issued or reacquired during the reporting period are weighted for the portion of the period they were outstanding.
- Earnings available to common stockholders: ((income from continuing operations [as it appears on the income statement]) + (net income)) − ((dividends declared on preferred stock) + (dividends accumulated on cumulative preferred stock))
- Weighted average shares outstanding does not include stock options or restricted stock until all conditions have been met or restrictions have been lifted.

Diluted EPS adjusts basic EPS by increasing the denominator to include additional shares outstanding if dilutive potential common shares (debt/equity instruments convertible into common shares, warrants, options, unvested stock, rights granted under employee share plans, and contingently issuable shares) have been issued, as determined by the treasury stock method:

(1) Assume all option awards/rights are exercised;

(2) calculate hypothetical proceeds received by company;

(3) include amount paid by employees, average unrecognized deferred compensation, and any tax benefits that would be credited to paid-in capital on exercise;

(4) assume hypothetical proceeds used to buy back shares on the open market at the average stock price for the relevant period;

(5) if options/awards were issued during the relevant period, average the market price from issuance to the end of period;

(6) (number of shares issued) − (assumed shares repurchased) = (net additional shares considered outstanding in diluted EPS calculation).

Chapter 3: Plan & Activity Details

Keeping track of what's going on with your plans is basically what you're there for. Even if you've got great systems in place, take a look through these to see if anything might be useful. *Remember to change templates as needed to fit your plan!*

To start, *"Corporate Information"* covers the information that governs the activity you're tracking. Keeping this with photocopies of all relevant source documents helps you and your department put your finger on key details whenever you need them—without having to wait for someone else to provide them to you first.

For your equity compensation planning, *"Stock Plan Basics"* helps you create a quick reference guide to the basic details of your stock plan. Then, "Nonqualified Compensatory Stock Options," "Incentive Stock Options," "Restricted Stock," "Restricted Stock Units," and "Stock Appreciation Rights" all provide you with overview information and key tax, accounting, and regulatory topics pertaining to each type of equity award for both the recipient and the employer corporation.

If you have an ESPP, *"Employee Stock Purchase Plan Basics"* helps you create a quick reference guide to its basic details. "Qualified Employee Stock Purchase Plans" covers the basic requirements for qualification under a 423 Plan ESPP as well as key tax, accounting, and regulatory topics for both the optionee and the employer corporation, and "Employee Stock Purchase Plans" covers the same optionee and employer corporation points for nonqualified ESPPs. And then, *"ESPP Offering Period Specifics"* helps you track basic details of each offering period.

"Basic Stock Pool Tracking" offers a basic method of simple tracking if you track manually (with or without a stock tracking software program in place). *"Stock Pool Tracking- Details"* and *"Stock Pool Tracking—Summary"* are more complex excel spreadsheets on the CD in the back of this book with formulas in place for both detail and summary tracking.

Once all these equity awards have been granted, people will probably eventually want to become shareholders. "Award Purchase Financing" provides some basics on the handling of different methods of payment for equity compensation. And *"In-House Equity Activity Checklist for Paper Tracking"* is just what it says—a way for you to make sure all the pieces of an exercise or sale have been processed.

And once you have shareholders, you'll need to maintain a stock register that tracks all of the shares of each class of stock, as well as a shareholder listing that gives cumulative totals of beneficial ownership of all classes of stock. Public companies might not maintain a spreadsheet in-house for this purpose, preferring instead to canvass brokers to compile lists electronically when needed. Private companies, however, don't have a whole lot of trading activity in their stock yet, and maintain pretty tight control over the share issuance process. *"Shareholder Equity"* and *"Stock Tracking"* are excel spreadsheets on the CD in the back of this book with formulas in place for those of you who track shares in-house.

Corporate Information

Much of this information can be found in your corporate documents or stock plan(s), but maintaining this information in one place can save a lot of reference time.

1. Full name of the corporation as stated on the articles of incorporation.
2. If the corporate name has been changed, to what and on what date did it become effective?
3. On what date was the corporation founded?
    a. Name(s) of founder(s).
4. In what state is the corporation incorporated?
    a. As of what date?

    ☐ **Attach a copy of the articles of incorporation**

5. How many total shares have been authorized for which classes?
6. (a-c) Have the articles of incorporation been amended? As of what effective date?

    ☐ **Attach a copy of the articles of incorporation, as amended**

7. (a-c) What classes of stock have been approved? How many shares are reserved? What was the original issue price? Are dividends to be paid?
8. The corporation's SIC code—full list available at www.sec.gov.
9. If a public company, what was the date of the public offering? How many shares were sold? At what offering price?
    a. Who was the underwriter for the IPO?
10. (a-c) Has the corporation experienced any merger, acquisition, or spinoff activity (circle relevant activity initial)? When? What was the name of the other entity involved? Are there other relevant details?

    ☐ **Attach summary documents.**

11. (a-c) Has the corporation experienced any stock splits? If so, when, in what ratio (forward or reverse), and were there any other relevant details?

    ☐ **Attach summary documents.**

*ATTACH: ☐ **Board of directors listing & contact information**
                ☐ **Compensation committee roster**
                ☐ **Audit committee roster**
                ☐ **Insider trading policy**

Corporate Information

1. Corporation name: _____
2. Name change to: _____ Date: _____
3. Date founded: _____
   a) Founded by: _____
4. State of incorporation: _____
   a) Date of incorporation: _____
5. Number of shares authorized / Class: _____
6. Amendments to articles of incorporation:
   a) Date: _____ Shares authorized: _____ Class: _____
   b) Date: _____ Shares authorized: _____ Class: _____
   c) Date: _____ Shares authorized: _____ Class: _____
7. Classes of Stock:
   a) Series: _____ Shares _____ Issue Price: _____ Dividends: _____
   b) Series: _____ Shares _____ Issue Price: _____ Dividends: _____
   c) Series: _____ Shares _____ Issue Price: _____ Dividends: _____
8. Corporation's SIC code/s: _____
9. Date of IPO: _____ Shares sold: _____ Offering price: _____
   a) Underwriter: _____
10. Merger/Acquisition/Spinoff Activity:
    a) M / A / S   Date: _____ Details: _____
    b) M / A / S   Date: _____ Details: _____
    c) M / A / S   Date: _____ Details: _____
11. Stock split activity:
    a) Date: _____ Ratio: _____ Details: _____
    b) Date: _____ Ratio: _____ Details: _____
    c) Date: _____ Ratio: _____ Details: _____

Stock Plan Basics

1. What is the name of this stock plan?

    a. ☐ **Attach a copy of the plan, with all forms and documents.**

2. When was this plan approved by the Board of Directors? By the shareholders?

    a. ☐ **Attach copies of the plan approvals.**

3. If your company is public, are the shares registered with the SEC? When was the form filed?

    a. ☐ **Attach copies of prospectuses, S-8s.**

4. On what date did the plan become effective?

5. On what date will the plan expire?

6. What is the aggregate amount of shares/units subject to the plan?

7. How can shares/units be added to this amount? By board approval? Shareholder approval? Is there an automatic renewal feature or evergreen provision?

8. What method(s) do you use to distribute stock plan information? Paper? If intranet/web site, what is the URL?

9. Who is the "Plan Administrator?" The board of directors? The management team?

10. Who is eligible to participate in this plan? All employees? All full-time employees? Directors? Contractors?

11. When will participants be eligible to receive awards? Immediately? After a waiting period of what length? Other timing constraints?

12. What is the maximum number of shares or units that may be granted to any one individual? Over what period of time?

13. What types of stock awards are allowed? Incentive stock options (ISO)? Nonqualified stock options (NSO)? Cash-settled stock appreciation rights (CSAR)? Stock-settled SAR (SSAR)? Reload options? Restricted stock awards (RSS)? Restricted stock units (RSU)? Phantom stock awards (PSA)? Employee stock purchase plan (ESPP)? Any others?

14. (a-b) Has the stock plan been amended? On what dates were approvals received?

    a. ☐ **Attach copies of any amendments.**

15. What is the standard term for an award granted under this plan?

16. What is the standard vesting period for an award granted under this plan?

17. What is the standard vesting schedule for an award granted under this plan?

18. Is deviation from these standards permitted? If so, to whom? To all employees or to a select group?

19. When is the fair market value established? Daily at the close of the day? Daily according to the opening price? Monthly? At each board meeting? Quarterly? Annually? What about on non-market days?

Stock Plan Basics—1 of 3

Plan: _____

1. Name of plan: _____
2. Plan approval dates: Board of directors: _____ Shareholders: _____
3. Shares registered with SEC? Y/N Date: _____
4. Plan effective date: _____
5. Plan expiration date: _____
6. Aggregate number of shares subject to plan: _____
7. Method for adding shares to the plan: _____
8. Plan information distribution method: Paper _____ Intranet/Web site _____
9. Plan administrator: _____
10. Eligible optionees: _____
11. Eligibility timing: Immediate _____ Waiting period _____ Other _____
12. Maximum aggregate individual grant _____ Over specified period _____
13. Award types allowed: ISO ____ NSO ____ CSAR ____ SSAR ____ Reload ____ RSS ____
    RSU ____ PSA ____ ESPP ____ Other _____ ____
14. Amendments to stock option plan:
    a) BOD approval: _____ Shareholders: _____ Details: _____
    b) BOD approval: _____ Shareholders: _____ Details: _____
15. Standard option term: _____
16. Standard vesting period: _____
17. Standard vesting schedule: _____
18. Deviation from standard vesting allowed? Y/N _____ If yes, to whom? _____
19. FMV determination timing: _____

20. How is the fair market value determined? Trading price? By the board of directors? By a CPA or outside firm? Some other method?

21. Does the plan allow awards to be granted at below fair market value? If yes, who determines the price? Is the price determined by using a formula or is it on a case-by-case basis?

22. When are option shares returned to the option pool? On expiration? Cancellation? Termination? Repurchase?

23. What payment methods are allowed by the plan? Cash? Loan/promissory note? Stock swap? Broker-assisted? Same-day sale? Any other methods?

24. How is the exercise date determined? The date of notice of exercise? The date of receipt of exercise payment? The date the exercise payment clears?

25. Are there any restrictions on exercise? For a private company, can options be exercised at any point or only when the company goes public or is acquired? Is there a mandated holding period after expiration for any or all optionees? Are there any limits to exercises?

26. Does your plan allow awardees to exercise/purchase unvested options/stock? All or only specified awardees?

27. If unvested stock is distributed, does your company retain the repurchase right until the stock has vested? If so, is the stock repurchased at the exercise price or at some other price?

28. Do you issue stock certificates for repurchasable shares? If so, is it held by the company (by whom and where) or by the shareholder?

29. Does your company retain a right of first refusal?

30. How are awards settled? Who gets to choose, employee or company?

    a. Cash: Which awards? (CSAR, PSA, etc.)

    b. Stock: Which awards? (SSAR, ISO, NSO, etc.)

31. For how long after termination can an employee exercise the award before it expires in the case of voluntary termination? Retirement? Involuntary termination? Disability? Death? Are there any other special cases?

32. Does this plan contain or have there been established any standard policies allowing for the acceleration of vesting in the case of voluntary termination? Retirement? Involuntary termination? The company's initial public offering (IPO)? Disability? Death? Change of control? Are there any other special cases?

    ☐ **Attach copies of policies.**

33. Does this plan contain or has a policy been established around the forfeiture of awards for any reason (such as subsequent employment with a competitor)?

    ☐ **Attach copy of policy.**

Stock Plan Basics—2 of 3

Plan: _____

20. FMV determination method: _____
21. Below FMV grants allowed? Y/N If yes, how is price determined? _____
22. Return to pool: _____
23. Payment methods allowed: Cash _____ Loan _____ Stock swap _____
    Broker-assisted _____ Same-day sale _____ Other _____
24. Exercise date determination: _____
25. Exercise restrictions: _____
26. Unvested stock exercise/purchase allowed? Y/N ____ If yes, by whom? _____
27. Does company retain repurchase right? Y/N____ If yes, at what price? _____
28. Delivery of repurchasable stock: _____
29. Does the company retain right of first refusal? Y/N ____
30. Award settlement: _____
    a) Cash: _____
    b) Stock: _____
31. Grant expirations on termination:

    Voluntary termination: _____   Retirement: _____

    Involuntary termination: _____   Disability: _____

    Death: _____   Other: _____

32. Vesting acceleration policies (check if policy is attached):

    Voluntary termination: ☐ _____   Retirement: ☐ _____

    Involuntary termination: ☐ _____   IPO: ☐ _____

    Disability: ☐ _____   Death: ☐ _____

    Change of control: ☐ _____   Other: ☐ _____

33. Option forfeiture policy: ☐ _____

34. Does this plan contain or has a policy been established for administration of a grant in the case of a leave of absence? Does vesting continue through the leave or does it stop and restart? For what types of leave?

    ☐ **Attach copy of policy.**

35. Does this plan contain or has a policy been established for administration of grants should a change of control occur? Will vesting accelerate? Will exercise restrictions be lifted?

    ☐ **Attach copy of policy.**

36. Are options granted under this plan assignable? If so, to whom? Spouses? Trusts? Members of the immediate family? Custodial accounts? Anyone?

37. Can income be deferred on exercise of an option? If so, through what process?

    ☐ **Attach copy of policy.**

38. What voting rights are assigned under this plan? Do optionees have any rights? Once shares have been purchased, when can they be voted?

39. What buyback provisions have been established?

    ☐ **Attach copy of policy.**

40. Has the company committed to an annual stock repurchase obligation under this plan? Is there a limit to the number of shares that may be repurchased? Over a certain period of time?

41. Who decides who will receive grants? How? All new hires? By seniority? Merit?

42. Who decides the amount of each award? Is the allocation done by formula? Is there a salary scale the grants are tied to?

43. How often are grants distributed? At hire? Annually? Quarterly by department?

44. How and by whom are dividends calculated?

45. When are dividends distributed?

46. To whom are dividends distributed?

47. Is there a minimum amount required for distribution?

Stock Plan Basics—3 of 3

Plan: _____

34. Leave of absence policy: ☐ _____
35. Change of control policy: ☐ _____
36. Are awards assignable? Y/N _____ If yes, by/to whom? _____
37. Can income be deferred on option exercise? Y/N If yes, how? _____
38. Voting rights: _____
39. Buyback policy: _____
40. Annual stock repurchase obligation: _____ Limitation: _____
41. Grant recipient determination: _____
42. Grant size determination: _____
43. Frequency of granting: _____
44. Dividend calculation: _____
45. Distribution Timing: _____
46. Dividend Recipients: _____
47. Minimum amount: _____

Nonqualified Compensatory Stock Options (NSOs)

A typical "nonqualified" or "nonstatutory" option gives the optionee the right to buy shares of company stock at a price determined at grant for a period of time into the future. Unlike incentive stock options, NSOs do not provide any special tax benefits to the optionee and are not "qualified" under Section 422. NSOs are governed by Internal Revenue Code (IRC) Section 83.

NSO—Optionee View

Option Grant
- Most compensatory options do not have a "readily ascertainable fair market value (FMV)" at the time of grant so no tax liability is incurred.

Option Exercise
- The date of exercise starts the holding period for capital gains tax treatment on sale unless an 83(b) filing has been made, in which case the date of vest starts the holding period. Note that an 83(b) election can only be made at exercise of unvested shares.
- The spread of the FMV over the exercise price is included in the optionee's gross income for the year and shows up on either the W-2 (employee) or 1099 (non-employee).
- The optionee's tax basis is the amount paid plus any compensation income reported.
- Withholding for applicable federal, state, and local taxes, Social Security, Medicare, and FUTA is required upon exercise of an NSO by an employee and can be paid in either cash or shares, as allowed by the company.

Disposition of NSO Stock
- When NSO shares (shares of stock received upon exercise of an NSO) are sold, the difference between the tax basis and the sale price is reported as capital gain.
- Stock held for one year or less results in "short-term" capital gain, which is currently taxed at ordinary income rates; stock held for more than one year results in "long-term" capital gain, which is taxed at more favorable rates.

NSO—Employer Corporation View

Option Price
- Current tax law places no limitations on the exercise price of an NSO, except that deferred compensation rules (IRC Section 409A) provide less favorable treatment for NSOs granted at less than FMV.
- For accounting purposes: under APB 25, if the option is granted at a discount from FMV, the amount of discount is treated as the intrinsic value of the option and amortized as a compensation expense over the service period. Under FAS 123R, the fair value must be measured at grant date and recognized over the service period.
- For pre-IPO companies, the FMV of the underlying stock should be reviewed and recalculated regularly to avoid cheap stock, deferred compensation, or other issues.

Option Grant
- Most compensatory options do not have a "readily ascertainable fair market value (FMV)" at the time of grant so there are no tax implications.
- If an option does have a "readily ascertainable FMV" (meaning the option is (1) transferable; (2) exercisable immediately in full; (3) not subject to restrictions having a significant effect on the option's value (vesting); and (4) the purchase FMV is readily ascertainable) at the date of grant, the option itself is property transferred as compensation, and the employer corporation recognizes a tax deduction equal to the amount of the compensation income recognized by the optionee.
- For accounting purposes: under FAS 123, the compensation expense incurred at grant of an NSO is determined by calculating the fair value of the option at grant date according to an approved option pricing model. Under APB 25, the compensation expense incurred at grant is equal to the intrinsic value of the option.

Option Exercise
- The spread of the FMV over the exercise price is included in the optionee's gross income for the year and reported on either the W-2 (employee) or 1099 (non-employee).
- Withholding for applicable federal, state, and local taxes, Social Security, Medicare, and FUTA is required upon exercise of an NSO.
- Stock can be used to pay tax withholding, but shares withheld for tax purposes create a accounting compensation expense unless the withholding is limited to the minimum amount due.
- The employer corporation is entitled to a tax deduction in the amount of compensation income reported by the optionee at exercise.
- Even if the optioned stock is issued by a parent or subsidiary of the optionee's employer, only the employer corporation is entitled to the tax deduction.

Administration
- Standard NSOs with no deferral features that are subject to taxation under IRC Section 83 and have an exercise price equal to the FMV of the underlying stock on the grant date are not subject to the deferred compensation provisions of IRC Section 409A.
- NSOs granted at a discount from FMV or with nonstandard terms or features may be subject to the deferred compensation provisions of IRC Section 409A.

Incentive Stock Options (ISOs)

An "incentive" (also called "statutory" or "qualified") stock option gives the optionee the right to buy shares of company stock at a price determined at grant for a period of time into the future. Tax benefits are available to the employee if certain rules are met and the option remains "qualified" as defined by Internal Revenue Code Sections 421, 422, and 424.

ISO Requirements

- **Holding periods.** A qualifying disposition of an ISO meets holding periods of two years from date of grant and one year from date of exercise. A disqualifying disposition fails to meet one or both criteria. (IRC 422(a)(1).)

- **Employment requirement.** The optionee must be in the continuous employ of the company or its subsidiaries from the date of grant until no more than three months before exercise—leaves not exceeding three months do not interrupt continuous employment; if re-employment is guaranteed by contract or statute, the employment relationship remains intact regardless of length of leave. (IRC 422(a)(2).)

- **Specified shares.** The plan must specify the aggregate number of either all types of shares or specifically ISO shares subject to it. A maximum as a percentage of shares authorized, issued, or outstanding on the date of adoption of the plan is acceptable. (IRC 422(b)(1).)

- **Eligible employees.** The plan must identify the employees or class of employees eligible to receive options. (IRC 422(b)(1).)

- **Shareholder approval.** The plan must have been approved by the company's stockholders within 12 months of adoption by the board of directors. (IRC 422(b)(1).)

- **Non-exclusion of ISO treatment.** The terms of the option must not provide that it will not be treated as an incentive stock option. (IRC 422(b).)

- **Grant date limitation.** The option may not be granted more than 10 years after plan adoption/approval. (IRC 422(b)(2).)

- **Exercise date limitation.** An ISO cannot be exercised more than 10 years after the date of grant. (IRC 422(b)(3).)

- **Exercise price.** The exercise price of an ISO must equal at least the FMV of the stock subject to the option at the time the option is granted. (IRC 422(b)(4).)

- **Nontransferability.** An ISO is not transferable and is not exercisable by anyone other than the optionee during the optionee's lifetime. (IRC 422(b)(5).)

- **10% owner.** If granted to a 10%+ owner, the ISO (a) cannot be exercised more than 5 years after the date of grant, and (b) must have a minimum exercise price of 110% of the FMV on the date of grant. (IRC 422(c)(5).)

- **$100,000 rule.** Only the first $100,000 (as measured at the time of grant) of FMV of stock subject to option that first becomes exercisable in any one calendar year retains its ISO status. Options that exceed that amount automatically lose ISO treatment. (IRC 422(d).)

- **Bankruptcy**. The transfer of an ISO share under title 11 or any other similar insolvency proceeding is not considered a disqualifying disposition of the ISO stock. (IRC 422(c)(3).)

- **Divorce**. The transfer of an ISO share to a former spouse incident to a divorce is not considered a disposition of the stock. (IRC 424(c)(4)(A).) The ISO stock transferred to a former spouse incident to a divorce is subject to the same tax treatment as before the transfer. (IRC 424(c)(4)(B).)

- **Disability**. In the case of an employee who is disabled, the optionee must be in the continuous employ of the company or its subsidiaries from the date of grant until no more than one year (extended from three months) before exercise. (IRC 421(c)(6).)

- **Death**. The ISO holding periods do not apply to an option exercised after the death of the optionee by the estate or beneficiary—any disposition of ISO stock exercised after death will be a qualifying disposition. (IRC 421(c)(1)(A).)

- **Modifications**. Certain modifications, such as to an ISO option or plan, may cause the option or plan to become "disqualified" and so lose ISO status. However, if an ISO option or plan is inadvertently modified so as to lose ISO status, then the modification is subsequently canceled before the earlier of option exercise or calendar year of modification, the ISO is not disqualified. (IRC 424(h)(1).)

- **Valuation**. Under the final ISO regulations issued in 2004, the FMV at grant (which bears on the minimum allowable option price as well as the $100,000 rule) may be determined "in any reasonable manner." The regulations give as an example taking an average of fair market values set by independent valuations. Short of having at least two independent valuations, experts are divided as to what would be acceptable.

ISO—Optionee View

Option Grant
- No tax liability is incurred at the time of grant.

Option Exercise
- The date of exercise starts the holding period for both ISO holding period requirements and capital gains tax treatment unless an 83(b) filing has been made, in which case the date of vest starts the holding period for capital gains treatment.
- No tax liability is incurred at the time of exercise of an ISO other than the alternative minimum tax (AMT).
- The regular tax basis is the amount paid to receive the stock.
- There is no required tax withholding upon exercise of an ISO.

Alternative Minimum Tax (AMT)
- The AMT requires taxpayers to make an alternate income tax calculation by not excluding certain deductions and exclusions they are entitled to in their regular income tax calculation, then comparing that amount with their regular income tax.
- The exercise of an ISO is a "tax preference item" requiring the AMT calculation unless the ISO was not vested at exercise and an 83(b) form has been filed.
- AMT is calculated on IRS Form 6251 and entered as a line item on IRS Form 1040.
- The spread on an ISO is among the items that must be included in the AMT calculation.
- If the amount owed under the AMT calculation is higher than the amount owed under the regular calculations, AMT is due. The amount paid that exceeds what would have been paid under the regular income tax calculation can be used as a credit in future years when the AMT would provide a tax liability lower than regular income tax.
- There is no way to determine what amount, if any, will be owed under the AMT until both regular income tax and AMT calculations are complete, but any time a significant ISO exercise takes place, a tax professional should be consulted to estimate how much money should be reserved for potential additional tax liability.
- AMT tax basis is the amount paid plus the AMT adjustment made. This means that when an employee has to pay an AMT adjustment on shares acquired under an ISO and not sold by the end of the tax year, the tax basis for future AMT calculations is increased by the amount of AMT paid at exercise of the ISO shares; for calculating the gain for ordinary income tax purposes, the basis remains the amount the employee had to pay to exercise the option.
- Estimated taxes should be calculated quarterly for the best results.

Qualifying Disposition of ISO Stock
- At disposition of the stock acquired by exercise of ISO stock, holding periods of two years from date of grant and one year from date of exercise have been met.
- The entire gain (exercise price to sale price) is taxed as long-term capital gain; if the sale price is less than the amount paid for the shares, no tax is due. Instead, there is a capital loss that may be used to offset ordinary income (up to $3,000) or future capital gains.

Disqualifying Disposition of ISO Stock

- At disposition of the stock acquired by exercise of ISO stock, holding periods of two years from date of grant and one year from date of exercise have *not* been met.
- If the sale price is less than the amount paid for the shares, a capital loss is recognized.
- If the sale price is less than the FMV at exercise but more than the amount paid for the shares, the gain is compensation income.
- If the sale price is more than the FMV at exercise, the spread (exercise price to FMV on the exercise date) is compensation income, any additional gain is capital gain.
- If the disposition is made in the same year as exercise, AMT reporting is not necessary.
- *If an 83(b) election has been filed for early exercise shares*, the spread between the exercise price and the FMV at the vesting date is recognized as compensation income at the time of vest, and the spread between the sale price and the FMV at the vesting date is capital gain.
- In all cases, brokerage fees or other selling costs are excluded from the calculation of ordinary income recognized.

ISO—Employer Corporation View

Option Price
- The exercise price of an ISO must be equal to at least the FMV of the underlying stock on the date of grant.
- In the case of a 10%+ owner, the exercise price of an ISO must be equal to at least 110% of the FMV of the underlying stock on the date of grant.
- For pre-IPO companies, the FMV of the underlying stock should be reviewed and recalculated regularly to avoid cheap stock or other issues.

Option Grant
- The grant of an ISO is of no tax consequence to the employer corporation.
- For accounting purposes: under FAS 123(R), the compensation expense incurred at grant of an ISO is determined by calculating the fair value of the option at grant date according to an approved option pricing model. Under APB 25, the compensation expense incurred at grant is equal to the intrinsic value of the option.

Option Exercise
- The exercise of an ISO is of no tax consequence to the employer corporation.
- The exercise of an ISO is an accounting nonevent to the employer corporation.
- The date of exercise starts the holding period for ISO holding period requirements.
- There is no required tax withholding upon exercise of an ISO, regardless of future disqualifying disposition.

Alternative Minimum Tax (AMT)
- The optionee, and not the company, is solely responsible for determining his or her AMT liability. There is no way to determine what amount, if any, will be owed under the AMT until both regular income tax and AMT calculations are complete—thus, there is no way for you to know for sure based on the transactional information available to you if AMT will be owed by the optionee since the AMT depends on so many other tax factors. Recommend consultation with a tax professional.

Qualifying Disposition of ISO Stock
- A qualifying disposition of ISO stock is of no tax or accounting consequence to the employer corporation.

Disqualifying Disposition of ISO Stock
- At disqualifying disposition of ISO stock, the employer corporation is entitled to a tax deduction in the amount of compensation income recognized by the optionee as a result of the exercise of the ISO stock.
- Even if the optioned stock is issued by a parent or subsidiary of the optionee's employer, only the employer corporation is entitled to a deduction.
- On disqualifying disposition, ISO stock is treated as NSO stock and may be subject to the deferred compensation provisions of IRC Section 409A (see **NSO Stock**).

Administration
- The employer corporation must send a statement of exercise to shareholders who have exercised ISOs on or before January 31 of the following calendar year, per IRC Section 6039.
- ISOs are not subject to the deferred compensation provisions of IRC Section 409A.

Restricted Stock Shares (RSS)

Under a restricted stock plan, shares are either awarded at no cost ($0), at par value, or purchased, but ownership is not transferred until vesting restrictions lapse.

RSS—Award Recipient View

Restricted Stock Shares—Vested
- If awarded shares are vested at receipt, the recipient must report compensation income in the amount of the fair value of the stock on the date of grant.
- If stock purchased is vested at the time of purchase, the recipient must report compensation income in the amount of the discount from FMV.
- The recipient's tax basis is the amount of compensation income reported.
- Withholding for applicable federal, state, and local taxes, Social Security, Medicare, and FUTA is required upon receipt of RSS by an employee and may be paid in cash, cash withheld from cash compensation, or shares, as allowed by the company.
- The holding period for capital gains tax treatment of a restricted stock award begins on the date of grant: for purchased shares the holding period begins on the date of purchase.
- Vested RSS confer all the rights of ownership as stock purchased on the open market.

Restricted Stock Shares—Unvested
- The receipt of an unvested restricted stock award is of no tax consequence to the recipient until the award vests unless an 83(b) filing has been made. If an 83(b) filing is made within 30 days of the award date, the recipient has elected to be treated for tax purposes as though the award was vested upon receipt (see above).
- As the award vests, the fair market value on the date of vest of the tranche of stock vesting must be reported as compensation income and will show up on either the W-2 (employee) or 1099 (non-employee).
- As the award vests, withholding for applicable federal, state, and local taxes, Social Security, Medicare, and FUTA is required and may be paid in cash, cash withheld from cash compensation, or shares, as allowed by the company.
- The recipient's tax basis is initially equal to the amount paid for the stock, then increases to include the amount of compensation income reported as each tranche vests
- The holding period for capital gains tax treatment begins for each tranche on the date of vest.
- Any dividends received on unvested restricted stock are treated as compensation, not dividends, and will show up on either the W-2 (employee) or 1099 (non-employee). If a timely 83(b) filing has been made, the dividends are treated as dividends.

RSS—Employer Corporation View

Award Ratios
- Restricted stock awards produce less equity dilution than stock options, but the proper award ratio depends on the stock price, volatility, and other factors and can only be determined by doing an option model.

Restricted Stock Grants
- For accounting purposes, the fair value of the stock is measured at the date of grant and expensed over the vesting period.
- For tax purposes, compensation income in the amount of either the fair value of the stock on the date of grant for stock awards or the discount from FMV for stock purchases is reported on either the W-2 (employee) or 1099 (non-employee).

Restricted Stock Share Delivery
- The employer corporation receives a tax deduction in the amount of the compensation income reported by the award recipient.
- Withholding for applicable federal, state, and local taxes, Social Security, Medicare, and FUTA is required upon receipt of vested restricted stock by an employee or as unvested restricted stock vests.

Dividends
- Any dividends paid on unvested restricted stock are treated as compensation, not dividends, and must be reported on either the W-2 (employee) or 1099 (non-employee).
- Dividends paid on restricted stock that has vested or for which a timely 83(b) election has been filed are reported on 1099-DIV.

Administration
- Standard restricted stock is not subject to the deferred compensation provisions of IRC Section 409A.

Restricted Stock Units (RSUs)

Restricted stock units are basically just restricted stock awards where the stock is not awarded until after vesting requirements have been satisfied. The future date of issuance is generally fixed at the time the RSUs are granted, typically upon termination of service or after a specified time, based on vesting or performance. 83(b) elections are not available for RSUs.

RSU—Award Recipient View

RSU Award
- The receipt of restricted stock units is of no tax consequence to the recipient until the award vests.
- Holders of RSUs have no voting rights.
- Holders of RSUs generally do not receive dividends, as they are not shareholders. They may receive dividend equivalents, as allowed by the plan.

RSU Vesting
- As the award vests, the fair market value on the date of vest of the tranche of stock vesting must be reported as compensation income and will show up on either the W-2 (employee) or 1099 (non-employee).
- As the award vests, withholding for applicable federal, state, and local taxes, Social Security, Medicare, and FUTA is required and may be paid in cash, cash withheld from cash compensation, or shares, as allowed by the company.
- The recipient's tax basis is initially $0, then increases to the amount of compensation income reported as each tranche vests.

RSU—Employer Corporation View

Award Ratios
- Restricted stock awards produce less equity dilution than stock options, but the proper award ratio depends on the stock price, volatility, and other factors and can only be determined by doing an option model. The value is similar to that of restricted stock, but may be lower if not dividend equalized.

RSU Award
- The award of restricted stock units is of no tax consequence to the issuing corporation until the award vests.
- For accounting purposes, the fair value of the stock is measured at the date of grant and expensed over the vesting period, less expected forfeitures, less projected tax benefits.

Share Delivery
- As the award vests, the employer corporation receives a tax deduction in the amount of the compensation income reported by the award recipient.
- Withholding for applicable federal, state, and local taxes, Social Security, Medicare, and FUTA is required upon receipt of stock by an employee. Withholding is commonly taken in the form of shares to result in a net delivery of shares after withholding.

Dividends
- Holders of RSUs generally do not receive dividends, as they are not shareholders. They may receive dividend equivalents, as allowed by the plan.
- Dividend equivalents paid on restricted stock units that have vested are reported on 1099-DIV.

Administration
- 83(b) elections are not available for RSUs.
- Holders of RSUs have no voting rights.
- Restricted stock units are subject to the deferred compensation provisions of IRC Section 409A.

Stock Appreciation Rights (SARs)

An SAR entitles its holder to a payment of either stock or cash that equals the amount by which shares of stock have appreciated in market value from a specified starting level to the date of exercise.

An SAR is not itself treated as "property" (so a grant is not taxed as a transfer of property) but as an unfunded and unsecured promise to pay either money or property in the form of stock, which in itself is not a taxable event. Once the SAR is exercised and settled, the method of payment determines the tax and accounting treatment.

SAR—Award Recipient View

SAR Grant
- The receipt of an SAR is of no tax consequence to the recipient until exercise.

SAR Exercise for Cash
- SARs settled in cash must be reported as compensation income and will show up on either the W-2 (employee) or 1099 (non-employee).
- Withholding for applicable federal, state, and local taxes, Social Security, Medicare, and FUTA is required and may be paid in cash, cash withheld from cash compensation, or shares, as allowed by the company.

SAR Exercise for Stock
- SARs settled in stock result in income in the amount of the fair market value of the stock on the date of exercise, which must be reported as compensation income and will show up on either the W-2 (employee) or 1099 (non-employee).
- Withholding for applicable federal, state, and local taxes, Social Security, Medicare, and FUTA is required and may be paid in cash, cash withheld from cash compensation, or shares, as allowed by the company.
- The tax basis of stock received as the result of the exercise of an SAR is the amount reported as compensation income.

SAR—Employer Corporation View

SAR Grant
- The grant of an SAR is of no tax consequence to the employer corporation.
- Holders of SARs have no voting rights.
- For accounting purposes: under FAS 123R, the fair value of a stock-settled SAR must be measured at grant date and recognized over the service period. If cash settlement of an SAR is allowed, then the grant must be treated as a liability award, with fair value measured and expensed at the time of vest.

Cash-Settled SARs—Taxation
- Once the SAR is exercised and settled, the method of payment determines the tax treatment; the employer corporation receives a tax deduction in the amount of the compensation income reported by the award recipient.
- Withholding for applicable federal, state, and local taxes, Social Security, Medicare, and FUTA is required on exercise by an employee.
- The IRS considers SARs exercisable for cash to be deferred compensation, which is taxed to the employee under IRC 61(a) and subject to the deferred compensation provisions of IRC Section 409A; any cash received is included in the recipient's gross income for the year.
- Currently, SARs granted pursuant to a program in effect on or before October 3, 2004 where the exercise price is not less than the FMV of the underlying stock on the grant date, and the SAR contains no deferral features, are not subject to the deferred compensation provisions of IRC Section 409A. In addition, SARs with fixed payment dates may not be subject to the deferred compensation provisions of IRC Section 409A.

Stock-Settled SARs—Taxation
- Once the SAR is exercised and settled, the method of payment determines the tax treatment; the employer corporation receives a tax deduction in the amount of the compensation income reported by the award recipient.
- Withholding for applicable federal, state, and local taxes, Social Security, Medicare, and FUTA is required upon receipt of stock by an employee. Withholding is commonly taken in the form of shares to result in a net delivery of shares after withholding. SARs which may be settled only in stock, have an exercise price equal to the FMV of the underlying stock on the grant date, have no deferral features, and where the underlying stock is publicly traded, are not subject to the deferred compensation provisions of IRC Section 409A.

Employee Stock Purchase Plan Basics

1. What is the name of this stock plan?

    ☐ **Attach copy of plan.**

2. When was this plan approved by the Board of Directors? By shareholders?

    ☐ **Attach copies of approvals.**

3. Does this plan meet all requirements under Internal Revenue Code Section 423?

4. On what date did the plan become effective?

5. On what date will the plan expire?

6. What is the aggregate number of shares subject to the plan?

7. How can shares be added to this amount? By board approval? Shareholder approval? Is there an automatic renewal feature or evergreen provision?

8. What method(s) do you use to distribute stock plan information? Paper? If intranet/web site, what is the path?

9. Who is the "plan administrator"? The board of directors? The management team?

10. (a-b) Has the stock plan been amended? On what dates were approvals received?

    ☐ **Attach copy(ies) of amendment(s).**

11. Who, if anyone, is excluded from participation in the plan?
    If this is a Section 423 plan, the only permissible exclusions are employees employed less than two years, whose customary employment is 20 hours or less per week, whose customary employment is for no more than five months in any calendar year, or highly compensated employees.

12. Does compensation include only base salary or also bonus compensation, commissions, overtime, lump-sum payments, etc.?

13. Is this plan funded through (after-tax) deductions from payroll? If yes, what is the maximum deduction amount allowed?

    ☐ **Attach a copy of the subscription/enrollment agreement.**

14. Are there any limitations on the number of shares that can be purchased during any offering period? Cap? Cap determined by formula? Maximum percentage of pay?
    If this is a Section 423 plan, the option grant may be made for no more than a total of $25,000 worth of stock for each calendar year in which the grant is outstanding, based on the FMV on the date of grant.

15. Does the plan allow for changes to be made in the participants' election percentages during an offering period? If yes, when are the changes allowed? At any time? Only at specified times? Are there any limitations on changes? Are both increases and decreases allowed?

16. How is the purchase price determined? At the time of grant? At the time of exercise? Whichever is lower? The lowest price at any time during the offering period?
    If this is a Section 423 plan, the price may not be less than 85% of the fair market value of the stock determined either at the date of grant or at the date of exercise.

Employee Stock Purchase Plan Basics

1. Name of plan: _____

2. Plan approval dates: Board of directors: _____ Shareholders: _____

3. Qualified 423 Plan? Y/N

4. Plan effective date: _____

5. Plan expiration date: _____

6. Aggregate number of shares subject to plan: _____

7. Method for adding shares to the plan: _____

8. Plan information distribution method: Paper _____ Intranet/website _____

9. Plan administrator: _____

10. Amendments to employee stock purchase plan:

    BOD approval: _____ Shareholders: _____ Details: _____

    BOD approval: _____ Shareholders: _____ Details: _____

11. Participation exceptions: _____

12. Includible compensation: _____

13. Payroll deduction plan? Y/N If Yes, maximum deduction allowed: _____

14. Purchase limitations: _____

15. Election percentage changes allowed? Y/N

    If Yes, when?: _____ Limitations?: _____

16. Pricing determination method: _____

17. Is the price rounded? If so, how?
18. How is the fair market value of the underlying stock defined?
19. What happens if a relevant date falls on a weekend or holiday?
20. What is the maximum length of any offering period?
    If this is a Section 423 plan, the maximum length is (a) five years if the option price may not be less than 85% of the FMV on the date of exercise, or (b) 27 months if the option price may be the lesser of 85% of the FMV on the date of grant or the date of exercise.
21. What is the standard length of any exercise period?
22. Does the plan allow for automatic withdrawal from any offering period? What triggers automatic withdrawal from the plan? Termination of employment? If the FMV of the underlying stock on any exercise date is lower than the FMV of the underlying stock on the date of grant (first day of the offering period)?
23. Does the plan allow for automatic enrollment in any offering period? What triggers automatic enrollment? Automatic withdrawal because of stock price?
24. Can participants be enrolled in more than one concurrent offering period?
25. How may participants withdraw from an offering period?

Employee Stock Purchase Plan Basics—2 of 2

17. Price rounding: _____

18. FMV definition: _____

19. Weekend/holiday policy: _____

20. Offering period maximum length: _____

21. Standard exercise period length: _____

22. Automatic withdrawal? Y/N Provisions: _____

23. Automatic rollover? Y/N Provisions: _____

24. Concurrent enrollment allowed? Y/N

25. Withdrawals: _____

ESPP Offering Period Specifics

1. On what date will the offering period start?
2. What is the deadline for enrollment/subscription in this offering period?
3. If the first day of the offering period falls on a weekend or holiday, what is the first effective date of the offering period—on which any date-relevant calculations are made or information recorded?
4. On what date will the offering period end?
5. What is the fair market value of the underlying stock on the first day of the offering period or on the day of calculation?
6. What discount from FMV is being offered to the participants?
7. How will the purchase price be calculated? Based on FMV at grant or exercise? At the lowest FMV during the offering period?
8. If the price has been rounded, from what to what?
9. For each exercise period, enter the purchase details: the purchase date, the price at which shares were purchased, and the total number of shares purchased (a-e).

    ☐ Attach a detailed list of the participants, the number of shares purchased for each participant, and total cost.

    ☐ Attach a detailed list of any participants who withdrew from participation, with dates.

ESPP Offering Period Specifics

1. Offering period start date: _____
2. Enrollment/subscription deadline: _____
3. Offering period effective date: _____
4. Offering period end date: _____
5. Offering date FMV: _____
6. Discount offered: _____
7. Price calculation: _____
8. Price rounding from: _____ to: _____
9. Purchase date/purchase price/number of shares purchased:

    a. _____ / _____ / _____
       ☐ Attached detailed list of participants/amounts.
       ☐ Attached detailed list of withdrawals.

    b. _____ / _____ / _____
       ☐ Attached detailed list of participants/amounts.
       ☐ Attached detailed list of withdrawals.

    c. _____ / _____ / _____
       ☐ Attached detailed list of participants/amounts.
       ☐ Attached detailed list of withdrawals.

    d. _____ / _____ / _____
       ☐ Attached detailed list of participants/amounts.
       ☐ Attached detailed list of withdrawals.

    e. _____ / _____ / _____
       ☐ Attached detailed list of participants/amounts.
       ☐ Attached detailed list of withdrawals.

Nonqualified Employee Stock Purchase Plans (ESPPs)

ESPPs may be qualified under IRC 423 or nonqualified; non-423 plan options are NSOs for tax purposes, and are governed by IRC Section 83.

Nonqualified ESPP—Participant View

Option Grant
- The date of grant is the first day of the offering period.
- No tax liability is incurred at the time of grant.

Option Exercise/Planned Purchase
- There is always an exercise/purchase date on which stock is purchased at the end of an offering period; there may be multiple exercise periods within a single offering period.
- The date of exercise starts the holding period for capital gains tax treatment.
- Payment of the exercise price is generally done through payroll deduction over the term of the offering period at a predetermined percentage of salary.
- Withholding for applicable federal, state, and local taxes, Social Security, Medicare, and FUTA is required upon exercise of an ESPP option and can be paid in either cash or shares, as allowed by the company.
- The spread of the FMV over the exercise price is included in the participant's gross income for the year and shows up on either the W-2 (employee) or 1099 (non-employee).
- The participant's tax basis is the amount paid plus the compensation income reported.

Disposition of Nonqualified ESPP Stock
- If the exercise price is not fixed at the date of grant at an amount at least equal to the FMV of the underlying stock, the spread (based on what the exercise price would have been if exercised on the date of grant) is taxed at ordinary income rates.
- The spread on the date of exercise is reported as compensation income, even if the sale is at a loss; the difference between the tax basis (amount paid plus compensation income) and the sale price is reported as capital gain.
- Stock held for one year or less results in "short-term" capital gain, which is currently taxed at ordinary income rates; stock held for more than one year results in "long-term" capital gain, which is taxed at more favorable rates.

Nonqualified ESPP—Employer Corporation View

Option/Purchase Price
- If the purchase price is calculated as a discount from fair market value, those ESPP shares do not qualify under Section 162(m) as tax-deductible incentive compensation above the $1 million limit.
- For accounting purposes: under FAS 123R, nondiscriminatory ESPPs with a maximum 5% discount and no look-back or similar features may be considered noncompensatory. Under APB 25, nondiscriminatory ESPPs with a maximum 15% discount may be considered noncompensatory regardless of look-back or similar features.

Option Grant
- The date of grant is the first day of the offering period.
- The grant of an ESPP option is of no tax consequence to the employer corporation.
- For accounting purposes: under FAS 123R, the compensation expense incurred at grant of an ESPP option is determined by calculating the fair value of the option at grant date according to an approved option pricing model unless the plan has been determined to be noncompensatory and thus of no accounting consequence to the employer corporation.

Option Exercise/Planned Purchase
- Payment of the exercise price is generally done through payroll deduction over the term of the offering period at a predetermined percentage of salary.
- The spread of the FMV over the exercise price is included in the participant's gross income for the year and reported on either the W-2 (employee) or 1099 (non-employee).
- Withholding for applicable federal, state, and local taxes, Social Security, Medicare, and FUTA is required upon exercise of an ESPP option.
- Stock can be used to pay tax withholding, but shares withheld for tax purposes create a compensation expense unless the number of shares withheld is limited to the number of shares with a fair value equal to the dollar amount of only the tax withholding.
- The employer corporation is entitled to a tax deduction in the amount of compensation income recognized by the participant.
- Even if the optioned stock is issued by a parent or subsidiary of the participant's employer, only the employer corporation is entitled to the tax deduction.

Administration
- Non-423 plan ESPP options may be subject to the deferred compensation provisions of the American Jobs Creation Act of 2004.

Adding Shares
- Pro-rata allocation is allowed if the share pool is depleted before the end of an offering period and no new shares are added.

Qualified Employee Stock Purchase Plans (423 Plan ESPPs)

ESPPs may be qualified under IRC 423 or nonqualified; options granted under a 423 plan are statutory options as defined in IRC sections 421, 423, and 424. Section 423 tax treatment is denied to all participants in an offering when any non-excludable employee is excluded or if one or more employees' shares must be denied 423 status because of some deficiency in the terms of their options.

Qualified 423 Plan Requirements

- **Holding periods.** (IRC 423a.1) A qualifying disposition of a 423 plan ESPP option meets holding periods of two years from date of grant and one year from date of exercise. A disqualifying disposition fails to meet one or both criteria.

- **Employment requirement.** (IRC 423a.2) The participant must be in the continuous employ of the company, its parent, or subsidiaries from the date of grant until no more than three months before exercise. Leaves not exceeding 90 days do not interrupt continuous employment; re-employment guaranteed leaves have no limit.

- **Employment requirement.** (IRC 423b.1) The plan must allow options to be granted only to the employees of the company adopting the plan or its related corporations;

- **Shareholder approval.** (IRC 423b.2) The plan must be approved by stockholders within 12 months of its adoption by the board.

- **5% shareholder exclusion.** (IRC 423b.3) The plan must not permit for options to be granted to any shareholder who owns, or would own immediately after the grant, 5% or more of the total combined voting power or value of the stock of the company.

- **Permissible exclusions.** The plan must allow participation to all employees except for those specifically allowed to be excluded: (1) (IRC 423b.4.A) those employed for less than two years; (2) (IRC 423b.4.B) those customarily employed for fewer than 20 hours per week; (3) (IRC 423b.4.C) those customarily employed for five months or less in the calendar year; and (4) (IRC 423b.4.D) highly compensated employees.

- **Equitable treatment.** (IRC 423b.5) The plan must by its terms provide that all participating employees shall have the same rights and privileges except that limitations may be placed on the basis of uniform applications such as salary and the plan may provide for a fixed maximum amount of stock that can be purchased by any one employee.

- **Exercise price.** (IRC 423b.6) The plan must not allow the exercise price of a 423 plan ESPP option to be less than the lesser than 85% of the FMV of the stock subject to the option at the time the option is either granted or exercised.

- **Maximum term.** (IRC 423b.7) The plan must provide for the maximum duration of options: (1) if the option is priced at less than 85% of the FMV at the date of exercise, it can be exercisable for no more than five years after the date of grant; or (2) options providing alternative exercise prices can be exercisable for no more than 27 months after the date of grant.

- **$25,000 cap.** (IRC 423b.8) The plan must prohibit each participating employee from purchasing stock under all 423 plans of the employer and related corporations to the extent that the FMV of stock measured at the date of grant would exceed $25,000 for each calendar year the options remain outstanding.

- **Nontransferability.** (IRC 423b.9) The plan must not allow for options to be transferable during the participant's lifetime.

- **Special Rule.** (IRC 423c) At qualifying disposition of a 423 plan ESPP option whose exercise price is less than the FMV at grant, the lesser of (1) the FMV at disposition less the exercise price, or (2) the FMV at grant less the exercise price, shall be recognized as compensation income.

- **Modifications.** (IRC 424h.2) At modification of a 423 plan option, the fair market value at grant will be the higher of (1) the FMV at original grant date; (2) the FMV on the modification date; or (3) the FMV at the time of any intervening modification.

423 Plan ESPP—Participant View

Option Grant
- The date of grant is the first day of the offering period.
- No tax liability is incurred at the time of grant.

Option Exercise/Planned Purchase
- There is always an exercise/purchase date on which stock is purchased at the end of an offering period; there may be multiple exercise periods within a single offering period.
- Payment of the exercise price is generally done through payroll deduction over the term of the offering period at a predetermined percentage of salary.
- The date of exercise starts the holding period for both capital gains tax treatment and 423 plan treatment.
- No tax liability is incurred at exercise.
- The participant's tax basis is the amount paid plus the compensation income reported at disposition.
- There is no required tax withholding upon exercise of a 423 plan option.

Qualifying Disposition of 423 Plan ESPP Stock
- At disposition of the stock acquired by participation in a 423 plan, holding periods of two years from date of grant and one year from date of exercise have been met.
- If the exercise price is not fixed at the date of grant at an amount at least equal to the FMV of the underlying stock, the spread (based on what the exercise price would have been if exercised on the date of grant) is taxed at ordinary income rates.
- The lesser of (1) the spread as of the beginning of the offering period; or (2) the gain realized on the sale of the stock, is compensation income.

Disqualifying Disposition of 423 Plan ESPP Stock
- At disposition of the stock acquired by participation in a 423 plan, holding periods of two years from date of grant and one year from date of exercise have *not* been met.
- If the exercise price is not fixed at the date of grant at an amount at least equal to the FMV of the underlying stock, the spread (based on what the exercise price would have been if exercised on the date of grant) is taxed at ordinary income rates.
- The spread on the date of exercise is compensation income, even if the sale is at a loss.
- The difference between the sale price and the FMV on the exercise date is reported as either capital gain or capital loss.
- Under the American Jobs Creation Act, possible issues in regard to Aggregate Supplemental Income may apply.

423 Plan ESPP—Employer Corporation View

Option/Purchase Price
- To remain tax-qualified: the exercise price of 423 plan stock must be no less than 85% of the FMV of the underlying stock on either (1) the date of grant or (2) the date of exercise.
- If the purchase price is calculated as a discount from fair market value, those ESPP shares do not qualify under Section 162(m) as tax-deductible incentive compensation above the $1 million limit.
- For accounting purposes: under FAS 123R, nondiscriminatory ESPPs with a maximum 5% discount and no look-back or similar features may be considered noncompensatory. Under APB 25, nondiscriminatory ESPPs with a maximum 15% discount may be considered noncompensatory regardless of look-back or similar features.

Option Grant
- The date of grant is the first day of the offering period.
- The grant of a 423 plan option is of no tax consequence to the employer corporation.
- For accounting purposes: the compensation expense incurred at grant of a 423 plan option is determined by calculating the fair value of the option at grant date according to an approved option pricing model unless the plan has been determined to be noncompensatory and thus of no accounting consequence to the employer corporation.
- To remain tax-qualified: no employee may purchase in any calendar year, under all 423 plans of the employer and related corporations, an aggregate total of more than $25,000 in stock measured by the FMV on the date of grant.

Option Exercise/Planned Purchase
- Payment of the exercise/purchase price is generally done through payroll deduction over the term of the offering period at a predetermined percentage of salary.
- The exercise of a 423 plan option is of no tax or accounting consequence to the employer corporation.
- The date of exercise starts the 423 plan holding period.
- There is no required tax withholding upon exercise of a 423 plan option.

Qualifying Disposition of 423 Plan ESPP Stock
- No tax deductions are available to employer corporations in connection with qualifying dispositions of 423 plan shares, even if an employee must claim part of the share price as ordinary income.

Disqualifying Disposition of 423 Plan ESPP Stock
- If a disqualifying disposition of 423 plan stock is made, the employer corporation is entitled to a deduction equal to the employee's realization of ordinary income.

Administration
- The employer corporation must send information statements to 423 plan participants on or before January 31 of the calendar year following the first transfer of legal title, per IRC 6039. Note that the first transfer of legal title does not mean on exercise, as for ISO shares, but the first transfer out of the name of the participant. This often happens on exercise when shares are transferred to street name by a broker, but if not, there must be a

tracking system in place to follow the shares until transfer of legal title at disposition of shares occurs—even and especially if the participant is no longer employed by the company.
- 423 Plan ESPP options are not subject to the deferred compensation provisions of the American Jobs Creation Act of 2004.

Adding Shares
- Pro-rata allocation is allowed if the share pool is depleted before the end of an offering period and no new shares are added.

Basic Stock Pool Tracking

1. Name of plan (official name of plan as well as your shorthand name for it).
2. How many shares were initially allocated to this plan for granting?
3. On what date were the shares first available for grant?

A. The date on which any activity recorded took place or became effective.
B. Fair market value (FMV) of the company's stock on that date.
C. Number of shares granted.
D. Number of shares canceled.
E. Number of shares returned to pool.
F. Any other activity you wish to record.
G. Number of shares left in the stock pool on the activity date.

To begin tracking, enter the date the plan became effective under A, and the number of shares approved under F and G on line 1. Now, for every date on which a change to the option pool is made, enter the relevant information and total under G.

*ATTACH: ☐ Copies of approved board and shareholder resolutions.
          ☐ Other supporting documentation (lists of new hires, terminations/cancellations, repurchases, etc.).

For example:
The plan is established (plan effective date) 1/1/04, with 300,000 shares available to grant. On 1/24/04, grants are approved totaling 123,400 shares at $3.00. On 6/27/04, grants are approved totaling 78,300 shares at $3.50, and 12,000 shares are canceled and returned to the pool because of an employee termination. On 1/16/05, 94,200 in grants are approved at $4.00, 11,400 are canceled and returned, and 13,100 are returned to the pool through repurchase of unvested shares. On 2/25/05, the board of directors approves the addition of 200,000 shares. On 5/14/05, the shareholders ratify the approval.

A. Activity date	B. FMV	C. Granted (-)	D. Canceled (+)	E. Returned (+)	F. Other	G. End Pool (=)
1/1/04					300,000 initial shares	300,000
1/24/04	$3.00	123,400				176,600
6/27/04	$3.50	78,300	12,000			110,300
1/16/05	$4.00	94,200	11,400	13,100		40,600
2/25/05					200,000 BOD addition	240,600
5/14/05					SH ratification	

Basic Stock Pool Tracking

1. Name of plan: _____

2. Initial number of shares available to grant: _____ 3. Date: _____

A. Activity date	B. FMV	C. Granted (-)	D. Canceled (+)	E. Returned (+)	F. Other	G. End Pool (=)

Equity Tracking Spreadsheets

If you are currently tracking your equity on spreadsheets in-house, you should really take a look at these. You should also really consider implementing a stock/option tracking program to save time and energy as well as eliminate many tracking errors.

If you outsource, use an equity tracking software program, or are at a large public company, just go ahead and skip right on over these pieces.

All of the spreadsheets provided here as pictures for you to look at are also provided for your use on the enclosed CD. Each file/workbook contains multiple worksheets—a template and sample of each spreadsheet. (Note: depending on your operating system configuration, your computer may not display filename extensions, so these files may appear as "options" and "shares" instead of "options.xlt" and "shares.xlt.")

Next pages—worksheets in the Excel file "options.xlt"

    Worksheet "pool":   Stock Pool Tracking—Summary
    Worksheet "options":   Stock Pool Tracking—Detail

Following Award Purchase Financing—worksheets in the Excel file "shares.xlt":

    Worksheet "common":   Stock Tracking—1 and 2
    Worksheet "preferred":   Stock Tracking—3
    Worksheet "shareholders":   Shareholder Equity

Stock Pool Tracking—Summary

[Company Name] STOCK OPTION POOL

Activity Date	FMV	Granted	Canceled	Exercised	Returned	Other	End Pool	Outstanding	Comments

[Company Name] Stock Option Plan Summary

Activity Date	FMV	Granted	Canceled	Exercised	Returned	Other	End Pool	Outstanding	Comments
2/2/03						5,000,000	5,000,000		initial shares
2003		7,500	4,000	0	500		4,997,000	3,000	
2004		12,250	4,000	100	0		4,988,850	11,150	

[Company Name] Stock Option Plan Detail

Activity Date	FMV	Granted	Canceled	Exercised	Returned	Other	End Pool	Outstanding	Comments
2/2/03						5,000,000	5,000,000		initial shares
3/3/2003	$0.10	4,500	0	0	0		4,995,500	4,500	
6/6/2003	$0.10	2,000	1,500	0	0		4,995,000	5,000	
9/9/2003	$0.10	1,000	2,500	0	500		4,997,000	3,000	
2/2/2004	$0.20	5,000	1,500	0	0		4,993,500	6,500	
7/7/2004	$0.20	3,750	2,500	0	0		4,992,250	7,750	
11/11/2004	$0.30	3,500	0	100	0		4,988,850	11,150	
4/4/2005	$0.30	1,500	5,000	0	0		4,992,350	7,650	
5/5/2005	$0.30	500	0	0	2,000		4,993,850	6,150	

The figures on this sheet tie back to the detail spreadsheet—you don't want to have to manually enter any information you don't have to—automate to reduce input errors! This summary provides you with many of the numbers you'll need to use in calculations for reporting purposes and makes it easy to check that your grants by date grouping have all been entered. This spreadsheet with formulas is on the enclosed CD.

Stock Pool Tracking—Detail (1 of 2)

[Company Name] STOCK OPTIONS

Light grey shading = terminated employee
Rose shading = notes to the data
Light blue shading = non-grant activity (exercises, cancellations, returns)
Red shading = needs attention

Activity Date	Grant Date	Grant #	Type	Optionee	Exercise Price	Shares Granted	Granted-to-Date	Shares From Grant #	Shares Exercised	Exercise Cost Paid	Shares Returned	Shares Canceled	Shares Remaining in Grant	Shares Outstanding
[Company Name] Stock Option Plan														
	3/3/2003	00001	ISO	Apple, A	$ 0.10	2,500								
	3/3/2003	00002	ISO	Bed, B	$ 0.10	1,500								
	3/3/2003	00003	ISO	Crown, C	$ 0.10	500								
3/3/2003						**4,500**			0	0	0	0	0	4,500
5/8/2003				Bed, B			1,500	00002				1,500	0	
	6/6/2003	00004	ISO	Daisy, D	$ 0.10	2,000								
	6/6/2003	00005	ISO	Eye, E	$ 0.10	2,500								
6/6/2003						**2,000**	6,500	00003	0	0	0	1,500	0	5,000
6/7/2003				Crown, C			500	00003			500	2,500	-2,500	
	9/9/2003	00006	ISO	Fish, F	$ 0.20	1,000	7,500							3,000
2003						**7,500**			**0**	**0**	**500**	**4,000**	**500**	**3,000**
11/11/2003				Daisy, D			2,000	00004				1,500	500	6,500
	2/2/2004	00007	ISO	Goose, G	$ 0.20	5,000	12,500					1,500	0	
7/2/2004				Eye, E			2,500	00005				2,500	0	
	7/7/2004	00008	ISO	Hat, H	$ 0.20	3,750	16,250					2,500	0	7,750
	11/11/2004	00009	ISO	Ice, I	$ 0.90	1,500								
	11/11/2004	00010	ISO	Jump, J	$ 0.90	3,500								
12/3/2004				Apple, A			2,500	00001	100	$ 10.00		0	2,400	
	11/11/2004					**3,500**	19,750		100	10	0	0	0	11,150
2004						**12,250**	**19,750**		**100**	**10**	**0**	**4,000**	**0**	**11,150**
2/6/2005				Goat, G			5,000	00007				5,000	0	
	4/4/2005	00011	ISO	Kite, K	$ 0.90	1,500	21,250					0	5,000	7,650
4/6/2005				Kite, K			2,000				2,000	0	0	
	5/5/2005	00012	ISO	Lowly, L	$ 0.90	500	21,750		0	0	2,000	0	0	6,150

Stock Pool Tracking—Detail (2 of 2)

KEY:

Activity Date:	Date on which non-grant activity took place
Grant Date:	Date of grant
Grant #:	Unique number assigned to grant
Type:	Type of grant (ISO/NSO)
Optionee:	Name of Optionee - preferably full name with middle initial
Exercise Price:	Exercise price of option
Shares Granted:	Number of shares granted
Granted -to-Date:	Totals: total number of shares granted-to-date under this plan / non-grant activity: number of shares in grant to start (original g
Shares From Grant #:	Non-grant activity: Grant # being referenced
Shares Exercised:	Number of shares being exercised
Exercise Cost Paid:	Total paid to exercise options
Shares Returned:	Number of shares returned to pool ungranted - if new hire approvals never start
Shares Canceled:	Number of shares canceled from awarded grants
Shares Remaining in Grant:	Non-grant activity: Number of shares left in grant after activity takes place
Shares Outstanding:	Total number of shares outstanding under this plan
Hire Date:	Date of hire by the company
Term Date:	Date of termination of employment / service
Expiration Date:	Date option expires
Vesting Start Date:	Date on which the option begins vesting
Vesting Schedule:	Rate at which the option vests

This spreadsheet is on the enclosed CD—obviously, it didn't all fit on the page easily in this picture format, and this book isn't printed in color (so everything appears in shades of gray), but you get the idea of how it works. The formulas are all in place, just make sure that if you use this and insert rows/columns, the formulas all still point to the right places when you're done. This is your detailed look at all stock option activity to date.

Award Purchase Financing

In practice, stock options are most often exercised at nonpublic companies by check or wire transfer, and at public companies through same-day sale arrangements. That said, equity award purchases can be financed using virtually any imaginable method allowed by the company, the plan documents, and securities regulations.

Any time shares are issued, be sure to have documentation on the exact name and form of the legal title into which the equity will be transferred, social security number, and address of the shareholder. Ensure that any required legends are included on the certificate that will be issued, and provide an explanation of their meaning and requirements thereof. If the shares are subject to statutory holding periods, ensure that the shareholder understands the difference between and consequences of qualifying and disqualifying dispositions. If the shares will be held in a brokerage account, make sure that you have contact information for the broker, and be sure to notify the broker of any statutory or regulatory restrictions on the shares.

Cash
Generally permitted in any one of a number of forms of payment (personal check, cashier's check, wire transfer, etc.) by the terms of most plans.

If the exercise is processed in-house, make copies of the check or transfer notification and attach to every set of exercise documents. Give the original to accounting with either one set of exercise documents or instruction on how to record. If NSOs are being exercised, calculate and collect the appropriate withholding amounts for applicable federal, state, and local tax, FICA, and FUTA purposes.

Same-Day Sale/Sell-to-Cover
The exercise of an option for stock in a public company using the proceeds from the sale of stock acquired under the option to pay both the exercise price and tax withholding, these transactions are generally executed through a brokerage. In a same-day sale, the entire option is exercised and liquidated with any proceeds over the exercise price and withholding going directly to the optionee. In a sell-to-cover, only the stock needed to pay the exercise price and withholding is sold; the rest of the shares are held by the shareholder. Even though a same-day sale constitutes a disqualifying disposition of ISO shares, ISO shares are not subject to withholding, per the American Jobs Creation Act of 2004.

If you have a captive broker, the process should be fairly routine and uneventful. The broker should have access to information allowing verification of options to expedite the process, copies of your exercise paperwork and pre-clearance policy if any, and any information needed to send exercise payment to the correct account. If you have optionees work directly with the broker, your main duties are to ensure that the records you are providing are as up to date as possible, to expedite the transfer of shares into the appropriate account, and to reconcile the figures the broker provides to you on a regular basis with your own records.

If you do not have a captive broker, your optionees work with any broker they choose, which is not recommended, due to compliance, communication, and taxation issues. In this case, you will receive the request to exercise and be prepared to process immediately, confirm the exercisability of options, ensure that all paperwork (including pre-clearance if applicable) is complete and accurate, coordinate the exercise payment, then arrange for the transfer of shares into the brokerage account.

The general consensus is that as long as the broker manages the method and timing of the sale appropriately, there is no restriction on executives under the Sarbanes-Oxley Act of 2002 prohibition on employer loans. Same-day sales are non-exempt for Section 16 purposes and must be reported on Form 4 by the end of the second business day following the transaction.

Immaculate Exercise
An immaculate exercise is effected by calculating the amount necessary to exercise the option in terms of the spread [(total exercise price) / (current FMV) = (number of shares to be surrendered)]. The optionee receives only the number of shares in excess of the shares surrendered as payment. If shares are used to pay tax withholding, remember that shares withheld for tax purposes create a compensation expense unless the withholding is limited to the minimum amount due. You need to be consistent with company policy and throughout your calculation as to the number of decimal points used in calculation and the method of rounding.

No exchange of money or previously owned shares is recognized. Your responsibility is to ensure that the correct amounts are recorded for accounting purposes, to update the option and share records, and to arrange for delivery of shares.

Stock Swap
Here, previously held stock is "swapped" at current FMV to exercise a stock option. The stock being swapped may be in the form of a physical certificate being surrendered, or may take place in much the same manner as an immaculate exercise, where only the new net shares over the number "surrendered" are actually issued; the old shares are "transferred" on the company's books. In this case, you need to properly document the transaction and effect the transfer.

If a physical certificate is exchanged, you must arrange for the cancellation and reissue of any remaining shares attributable to that certificate, as well as for the issue of a new share certificate for the optioned shares. If the certificate is not available (usually because the shareholder in a nonpublic company has lost it), you must arrange for proper documentation by attestation, where the shareholder signs forms to say that the certificate has been lost or destroyed and will never be produced. If the shares are held in a brokerage account, no certificate cancellation or reissue is necessary if the broker can attest to the holding of the shares.

On exercise of NSOs, the shares being submitted constitute a tax-free exchange for the same number of "exchange" shares and retain the original shares' tax basis; the shares received in excess are "added" shares received for zero payment, generate compensation income in the year of exchange (or when they vest, if unvested), and have a basis equal to the taxable income reported. The surrender of ISO shares to exercise an NSO does not constitute a disqualifying disposition of the ISO shares.

On exercise of ISOs, the shares being submitted constitute a tax-free exchange for the same number of "exchange" shares and retain the original shares' tax basis; the shares received in excess are "added" shares and have a basis equal to the amount of cash used to exercise the option (normally, but not always, zero). Both sets of ISO shares are subject to the holding period rules to determine their taxation pursuant to qualifying disposition rules. The surrender of ISO shares to exercise an ISO can be a disqualifying disposition if ISO shares that have not yet met the holding period requirements are used; the surrender of restricted shares to exercise an ISO is a taxable disposition of the restricted shares. In any case, when executing the exercise of an ISO through a stock swap, it is wise to have your optionee/shareholder consult with the appropriate advisors about the status of this bifurcated tax basis.

Stock Option Pyramiding
This is essentially a sell-to-cover using a stock swap, where the optionee exercises a portion of a stock option, then immediately resubmits the shares received to exercise the option on the remaining shares under the same option. The pyramiding transaction is treated for accounting purposes as an SAR settled in shares. A "phantom" pyramiding can also be effected, where the optionee retains the shares being "submitted," and the company issues a certificate for only the net shares.

Stock Option Gain Deferral/"Rabbi Trust"
A "rabbi trust" is an irrevocable trust created as a vehicle for tax deferral of ordinary income associated with the exercise of in-the-money NSOs.

Generally, the employee tenders mature shares with a FMV equal to the aggregate exercise price of the stock options being exercised. The employer issues new shares equal to the number of the mature shares tendered. The remaining shares under the option being exercised are called "deferred option shares" and are credited to the employee's account in a deferred compensation plan denominated in stock, stock units, or cash value of deferred option shares. Distribution is made at some time in the future, generally upon retirement or termination.

During the deferral period, employees are typically not permitted to vote or receive dividends on deferred shares; the deferred shares are merely a contractual obligation of the employer, not secured or evidenced by notes in any way; if the funds are needed to protect the company from creditors, they are available for this purpose. This risk of the loss of the benefit is considered sufficiently significant that the employee has not constructively received the benefit (and hence been taxed) at the time of deferral.

Most U.S.-based rabbi trusts are not affected by the provisions of the American Jobs Creation Act of 2004.

Employer Loans
Under the Sarbanes-Oxley Act of 2002, loans to company insiders, as defined by the SEC, are prohibited. The same-day-sale process has been scrutinized due to a belief that the settlement process might represent a loan to the seller, but if handled properly by the brokerage, the same-

day-sale process should not be a Sarbanes-Oxley issue. Any purchase of equity compensation using an employer loan must be done by non-insiders, and any such loans must be paid in full before the employee's designation as a Section 16 insider if such promotion should occur.

Some stock plans contain provisions that on occurrence of certain events such as continued employment, vesting, or a stock price lower than the exercise price, a loan previously granted will be forgiven; loan terms can also provide for ratable forgiveness over the term, where if the employee terminates prior to maturity of the loan, any shares related to the portion of the loan not forgiven will be returned to the company. Reference your plan when reading over the terms of an employer loan used to purchase equity compensation.

The purchase of equity compensation with a company loan should be handled by you as similar to a purchase made using cash. The promissory note as well as any evidence of collateral should be filed with exercise paperwork.

Below-market loans on the basis of insufficient stated interest terms (e.g., one charging a specified amount of simple interest) have their principal recharacterized by the IRS and adequate interest calculated based on new principal. As a result, the employee is deemed to have paid less than FMV for the stock at exercise. An ISO exercised in this way is disqualified and characterized as an NSO. An NSO exercised in this way reduces the employee's basis in the stock by the imputed interest amount.

A recourse note is a promissory note where the employer has recourse to all or substantially all of the employee's substantive assets and would intend to enforce that right in the event of default by the employee. Both capital gains and Rule 144 holding periods begin upon receipt of a recourse note.

A nonrecourse note is a promissory note where the employer has no recourse to the employee's assets beyond the collateral provided. The stock is not considered transferred until the note is fully paid or collateralized. If the note is collateralized solely by the underlying stock, the capital gains holding period begins for tax purposes. Once collateral for the amount of the note in addition to the underlying stock is received, the Rule 144 holding period begins.

A recourse note can be viewed as nonrecourse if the employer would not intend to seek repayment beyond foreclosing on the collateral or if it has historically not demanded repayment of loan amounts in excess of collateral. Check with your legal counsel on the characterization of the note and the holding period start date before any distribution of stock subject to Rule 144.

Stock Tracking (1 of 3)

[Company Name] COMMON SHARE REGISTER

CERT #	Legends	Issue Date	Share Certificate Issued To:	# of Shares Issued	Current Shares	Shares From	Acquisition Date	Price Per Share	Acquisition Cost	Cancel Date	Reissued As
1		8/8/2000	Big Family	20,000	0	Treasury	01/01/00	$1.50	$30,000.00	03/03/01	3,4
2		8/8/2000	Lotta Money	20,000	20,000	Treasury	01/01/00	$1.50	$30,000.00		
3		3/3/2001	Big Family Living Trust	10,000	10,000	1	01/01/00		$0.00		
4		3/3/2001	Big Family, Jr.	10,000	10,000	1	01/01/00		$0.00		
5		2/2/2002	Terminated Consultant	500	500	Treasury	02/02/02	$1.50	$750.00		
6		4/4/2004	Terminated Employee	104	104	Treasury	04/04/04	$1.50	$156.00		
			Total Common Shares		40,604				$60,906.00		

KEY:

	Certificate cancelled
CERT #	Certificate number
Legends	Class of stock issued
Issue date	Date certificate issued
Issued to	Name as shown on certificate
# of shares issued	Number of shares as shown on certificate
Current shares	Number of shares currently held in certificate form
Shares from	Origin of shares: if from a surrendered certificate, certificate number; otherwise, Treasury
Acquisition date	Date for shareholder's holding basis
Exercise cost	Amount paid to acquire stock
Cancel date	Date certificate cancelled
Reissued as	Certificate numbers replacing this cancelled certificate
Repurchase rights	Does the company retain repurchase rights on this stock? If so, see below
Comments	Any comments you'd like to make about the transaction
Signature by	Person signing purchase agreement
Title	Title of person signing in role of purchaser
Entity	If not an individual, name of entity purchasing shares
Description	If not an individual, description of entity purchasing shares
Address	Street address of shareholder
City	City of shareholder address
State	State of shareholder address
Zip	Postal code of shareholder address
Telephone	Shareholder telephone
Fax	Shareholder fascimile number
Email	Shareholder email address

Stock Tracking (2 of 3)

[Fiscal/Calendar] Year Totals		shares issued		acquisition cost
	2000	40,000		$60,000.00
	2001	0		$0.00
	2002	500		$750.00
	2003	0		$0.00
	2004	104		$156.00
		40,604		$60,906.00

Repurchasable Shares

	issue date		shares issued	repurchasable		repurch.price	repurch.cost
5	2/2/2002	Terminated Consultant	500	500	Treasury	$1.50	$750.00
		repurchase right lapses at 25% per year for four years					
	2/2/2003			375		$1.50	$562.50
	2/2/2004			250		$1.50	$375.00
	2/2/2005			125		$1.50	$187.50
	2/2/2006			0		$1.50	$0.00

Here you're tracking just common stock—which means you're also tracking option exercises. You also can use this to accurately track annual totals as well as repurchasable shares. This spreadsheet with formulas is on the enclosed CD.

Stock Tracking (3 of 3)

[Company Name] PREFERRED SHARE REGISTER									
CERT #	Class	Issue Date	Share Certificate Issued To:	# of Shares Issued	Current Shares	Shares From	Acquisition Date	Acquisition Cost	Cancel Date	Reissued As

SERIES A PREFERRED										
PA-1	Series A	1/1/2000	Big Family	60,000	0	Treasury	01/01/00	$180,000.00		
PA-2	Series A	1/1/2000	Lotta Money	25,000	25,000	Treasury	01/01/00	$75,000.00	03/03/01	PA-3
PA-3	Series A	3/3/2001	Big Family Living Trust	30,000	30,000	PA-1	01/01/00	$0.00		
PA-4	Series A	3/3/2001	Big Family, Jr.	30,000	30,000	PA-1	01/01/00	$0.00		
			Total Series A Preferred		85,000					

SERIES B PREFERRED									
PB-1	Series B	7/7/2002	Investment Company	3,000,000	3,000,000	Treasury	07/07/02	$15,000,000.00	
PB-2	Series A	7/8/2002	Lotta Money	25,000	25,000	Treasury	07/08/02	$125,000.00	
PB-3	Series A	7/9/2002	Big Family Living Trust	30,000	30,000	Treasury	07/09/02	$150,000.00	
PB-4	Series A	7/10/2002	Big Family, Jr.	30,000	30,000	Treasury	07/10/02	$150,000.00	
			Total Series B Preferred		3,085,000				

SERIES C PREFERRED									
PC-1	Series C	5/5/2004	Lotta Money	25,000	25,000	Treasury	5/5/2004	$50,000.00	
PC-2	Series C	5/5/2004	Big Family Living Trust	50,000	50,000	Treasury	5/5/2004	$50,000.00	
PC-3	Series C	5/5/2004	Big Family, Jr.	50,000	50,000	Treasury	5/5/2004	$100,000.00	
PC-4	Series C	5/5/2004	Investment Company	2,000,000	2,000,000	Treasury	5/5/2004	$4,000,000.00	
			Total Series C Preferred		2,125,000				
			TOTAL PREFERRED SHARES		5,295,000				

And finally, depending on how much activity you have, you can track all of your preferred shares on one worksheet or separate it out by class. This spreadsheet with formulas is also on the enclosed CD.

Shareholder Equity

[Company Name] SHAREHOLDERS *updated through [Certificate Number]*

Shareholder	Common	%	Series A	%A	Series B	%B	Series C	%C	TOTAL	%
Company, Investment		0.00%		0.00%	3,000,000	97.24%	2,000,000	94.12%	5,000,000	93.71%
Consultant, Terminated	500	1.23%		0.00%		0.00%		0.00%	500	0.01%
Employee, Terminated	104	0.26%		0.00%		0.00%		0.00%	104	0.00%
Family, Big	20,000	49.26%	60,000	70.59%	60,000	1.94%	100,000	4.71%	240,000	4.50%
Family Jr., Big			30000		30000		50000			
The Big Family Living Trust			30000		30000		50000			
Money, Lotta	20,000	49.26%	25,000	29.41%	25,000	0.81%	25,000	1.18%	95,000	1.78%
TOTALS	**40,604**	**100.00%**	**85,000**	**100.00%**	**3,085,000**	**100.00%**	**2,125,000**	**100.00%**	**5,335,604**	
									5,335,604	**100.00%**

KEY:

	Amounts shown in horizontal pattern bars are detail breakdowns of controlled shares and are not used in calculation.
	Format row as text to keep the numbers from being counted. (in the vertical columns it's just to make it easier to read)
	Sum of totals in the vertical column
	Sum of totals in the horizontal row
Shareholder:	Shareholder Name
Common:	Number of shares of common stock beneficially owned
%:	Percentage ownership of common stock
Series A:	Number of shares of Series A stock beneficially owned
%A:	Percentage ownership of Series A stock
Series B:	Number of shares of Series B stock beneficially owned
%B:	Percentage ownership of Series B stock
Series C:	Number of shares of Series C stock beneficially owned
%C:	Percentage ownership of Series C stock
TOTAL:	Total number of shares beneficially owned
%:	Total percentage of company ownership

Preparing for your closely held company's annual meeting, it's important to know who owns what and in what percentage. This spreadsheet with formulas is on the enclosed CD.

Equity Activity Checklist

- For every equity transaction, attach a copy of this checklist.
- For each item, either check off upon completion or enter the date completed.

1. Name as shown on grant document.
2. Social Security number/taxpayer identification number.
3. Date transaction was initiated / date all transactional items completed.

4. What is the control number of the grant involved?
5. Complete the details for the grant involved.

6. Is this an exercise transaction?
7. Is this a same-day sale or cashless exercise transaction as well?

8. What trade number has this been assigned?
9. What is the broker account number?
10. Who is the broker involved? Include contact information for the person with whom you are communicating.

11. Did you verify that the number of shares requested is available/vested?
    - ☐ Attach copy of printout.
12. Did you receive a completed exercise agreement from the optionee?
13. *(Section 16 Insider)* Have you completed certification, signoff, and/or 144 paperwork?
14. Exercise transaction: If exercise amount paid by cash or other method, complete this section.
15. Exercise transaction: If same-day sale/cashless exercise, complete this section.
16. Generate activity confirmation and distribute to all parties.
17. Don't forget to request funds.
18. Once funds are received, file copy and route appropriately.
19. Have shares been issued in a timely fashion?
20. *(Section 16 Insider)* Have you filed the Form 4?

Equity Activity Checklist

1. Name: _____
2. SSN/TIN: _____
3. Transaction initiation date: _____ Completion date: _____

4. Grant control number: _____
5. Grant date _____ Exercise price _____ Shares granted _____

6. ____ Exercise   _____ shares at $____/share
7. ____ Sell   _____ shares at $____/share

8. Trade number: _____
9. Broker account number: _____
10. Broker/contact person: _____

11. ____ Verified number of available/vested shares (print and attach report).
12. ____ Received completed exercise agreement from employee.
13. ____ *Section 16 officer/director*
    a. ____ *Insider certification completed.* _____
    b. ____ *Compliance officer signed off.*
    c. ____ *Completed Rule 144 paperwork with broker.*
14. ____ Received exercise payment. _____
    a. ____ Copy of check filed. ____ Original check sent to accounting. _____
    b. ____ Other payment method: _____
15. ____ Same-day sale/cashless exercise
    a. ____ Called broker with verbal SALE info based on employee's request.
    b. ____ Faxed confirmation to broker.
    c. ____ Received broker confirmation of sale price.
    d. ____ Logged into internal tracking.
    e. ____ Printed activity confirmation from internal tracking.
    f. ____ Notified employee of sale info.
16. ____ Distributed activity confirmation to employee _____
    a. ____ ... to file
    b. ____ ... to accounting/payroll (for W-2 or 1099 inclusion).
17. ____ Sent fax to broker requesting funds with confirmation showing amount due.
18. ____ Received check from broker: _____
    a. ____ Copy of check filed. ____ Original check sent to accounting. _____
19. ____ Instructed transfer agent to issue shares to employee/broker. _____
20. ____ *Section 16 Officer/Director: Filed Form 4*

Chapter 4: Section 16

Yes, Section 16 compliance technically falls under "Plan & Activity Details," but it just felt like it merited its own section—especially since the people affected are the ones most likely to have a say in your annual bonus!

Even though responsibility for Section 16 and other insider issues is generally shared between multiple people including a compliance officer who is probably not you, you probably are or will be at some point responsible for at least the Form 3/4/5 filing. "Section 16 Filings" gives an overview of some of the key points of section 16 filings, and "EDGAR" discusses some of the key points of filing via EDGAR.

As you look that information over, you'll realize that you need to have certain key pieces of information about your Section 16 officers before you can do anything. *"Section 16 Officer—Initial Information Capture"* helps you collect and standardize the information you'll need about each of your reporting insiders.

And every time you need to provide executive and director compensation details, you'll need to make sure they're current. *"Section 16 Officer—Stock Holdings"* gives you a basic format for first collecting then regularly querying your insiders about their ownership interest in company equity instruments.

Section 16 Filings

Form 3—Initial Statement of Beneficial Ownership of Securities.
Used to disclose the fact that a person has become a Section 16 insider.
Filing frequency: once—each time an individual becomes subject to Section 16 reporting.
Filing deadline: within 10 days after the event making the person an insider or by the effective date of the initial registration statement.
File with: the SEC, the company, and the exchange on which the company's stock is traded.
Report includes: detailed information on the insider's direct and indirect stock holdings, as well as any stock options, warrants, rights, and convertible stocks or bonds.

Form 4—Statement of Changes in Beneficial Ownership of Securities.
Used to disclose any non-exempt change and many exempt changes in the Section 16 insider's ownership of company stock.
Filing frequency: periodic.
Filing deadline: on or before the second business day after either the day on which a change in beneficial ownership has occurred (the execution date), or the day on which the insider is notified that a change in beneficial ownership has occurred (the deemed execution date) of transactions qualifying for a delay in filing.
File with: the SEC, the company, and the exchange on which the company's stock is traded.
Standard reportable transactions include: open market purchases and sales, option exercises, option and stock grants, option and stock awards, repricings, option exchanges, discretionary transactions in qualified retirement plans, and sales of securities to the company.
Delay qualified transactions include: discretionary transactions as described in Rule 16b-3 (fund transfers and early distributions in tax-conditioned plans, such as 401k, profit-sharing, pension, and other qualified retirement plans), and transactions in accordance with Rule 10b5-1 plans where the timing of transactions is determined by factors outside of the insider's control.

Form 5—Annual Statement of Changes in Beneficial Ownership of Securities.
Used to report any transactions that are reportable but are not required to be reported on Form 4. Also can be used to report holdings and/or changes not previously reported on Forms 3 or 4 on a delinquent basis.
Filing frequency: annual.
Filing deadline: if required, must be filed within 45 days after the end of the issuer's fiscal year.
File with: the SEC, the company, and the exchange on which the company's stock is traded.
Transactions include: gifts, transfers due to bequest or inheritance, and small acquisitions as defined in Rule 16a-6.

Reporting Persons
Those directors or officers designated Section 16 officers ("insiders") with board of directors approval and those with 10% or greater holding of company stock are required to comply with Section 16 filing requirements. Any designation must be documented in board meeting minutes. Complete the *Section 16 Officer—Initial Information Capture* for each insider to be sure that you have all relevant information on file.

In addition, any company stock held by your insiders through indirect holdings such as trusts, partnerships, family members, or other entities, creates a reporting requirement. Make sure that you have contact information for any indirect holdings, and require that your insider notify all relevant parties of their Section 16 reporting requirements.

Although the reporting requirement and any penalties for improper reporting are the responsibility of the individual, most companies provide significant assistance to lessen the chance of problems.

Blackout Periods
Section 16 insiders are prohibited from trading in company stock during certain designated periods, generally a specified number of days immediately before and immediately after the release of any financial or material information about the company. The blackout periods should be established by your compliance officer and communicated to you and to any affected parties with adequate notice. Rule 10b5-1 of the Securities Exchange Act of 1934 establishes guidelines for written plans for trading securities at predetermined intervals, not subject to blackout period restrictions on insider trading. And some transactions such as option grants that are not subject to blackout periods are nonetheless subject to filing requirements, so do not let blackout periods keep you from monitoring Section 16 activity.

Power-of-Attorney
Many companies, especially in light of the two-day filing deadline, require their insiders to complete a Power-of-Attorney form authorizing one or more company representatives to sign Section 16 filings on their behalf. The Power-of-Attorney must be included with the first filing utilizing it, but then is not required unless it expires, in which case the new POA must be included with the first filing requiring it. Regardless, have the insider sign the Form being filed whenever possible, and if the POA is utilized, have the insider sign the Form after the fact for retention in the company's files.

Brokers
Your insiders may have a huge range of brokers with whom they do business, but your work life as it relates to reporting and compliance will be immensely simplified if your company chooses to require your insiders to use a broker with whom you have established a relationship for all trades in company stock. If you allow your insiders to work with a broker of their choice, they must give you all contact information for everyone they work with at their broker. In addition, you should require that they complete, sign, and provide you with copies of any releases necessary to allow their broker to report all transactions in company stock to the company.

Whether you have a captive broker in place or work with a different one for each insider, you will need to contact each broker in advance of any transactions to review their reporting procedures and ensure that you will receive timely notification of any reportable transactions to meet filing requirements. Most brokerages will have electronic notification systems in place to alert you as soon as a trade takes place but no later than the day following the transaction. If a trade takes place over multiple days, make sure that you will be notified as soon as each piece of a trade is executed to avoid delinquent filings.

Assuming you have a pre-clearance policy in place, any broker you work with should receive a copy of the policy and agree to abide by its terms.

Pre-Clearance Policy
Many companies have pre-clearance policies to require that insiders obtain approval for any trades in company stock before actually trading. This makes compliance with securities laws such as Rule 144 much easier, prevents insiders from inadvertently triggering Section 16(b) short-swing profit recovery, prevents trades that might not be in the insider or company's best interests, and gives you advance notice of Form 4 filing. All requests should be in writing and should include the number of shares and the nature of the transaction. Responses should also be in writing and should occur no more than 24 hours after the request. Approved trades should take place within a specified period, usually no more than a few days, or the approval will expire and the request must be resubmitted. Obviously, an executed trade should be reported to you as soon as possible after the trade and no later than the end of the day on which the trade occurred to facilitate reporting.

Transaction Details
The information you will receive as notification of a reportable transaction should include: the date(s) of execution, execution price, and the number of shares exchanging hands at each price. Transactions that are not subject to short-swing profits recovery must be reported, but it is a good idea to footnote their exempt status. If the transaction qualifies for delayed reporting, report the execution date in a footnote.

Ideally, completed Form 4s should be reviewed by the insider and the compliance officer before filing. If this is not possible and errors are discovered after filing, an amended filing must be made to correct errors. If material errors are discovered after filing, the amended filing will be considered a delinquent filing.

Filing of all Forms 3, 4, and 5 is done via EDGAR (see below).

Filing Responsibility
The responsibility for filing Section 16 reports technically falls to the reporting person, but in practice most companies file Section 16 reports as a courtesy to their insiders and to avoid noncompliance with reporting requirements that would have to be reported to and by the company. So, the person with "responsibility" for filing via EDGAR is generally the stock plan administrator or company compliance officer.

Be sure to have a backup plan in case the primary person with responsibility for filing via EDGAR is unavailable. With the two-day filing deadline, having someone out sick is no excuse for not filing a required form on time, but can happen if only one person is responsible for filing. There should be multiple people in the loop on all time sensitive transactions.

Forms 3, 4, and 5 support phone numbers

General Filer Support Number
Office of Filings and Information Services _____ (202) 942-8900
  Branch of Filer Support (fax Form ID here)_____ fax (202) 504-2474

Rule Interpretations
Division of Corporate Finance, Office of Chief Counsel _____ (202) 942-2900

Electronic Filing Questions
(includes accidental filing of the same report more than once)
Office of EDGAR and Information Analysis _____ (202) 942-2940

Filing Date Adjustments   _____fax (202) 942-9542

EDGAR

SEC's Electronic Data Gathering, Analysis, and Retrieval system, through which companies electronically file reports and registration statements, EDGAR is used for filing Forms 3, 4, and 5 as well as to search for basic company and insider information, and real-time company and individual filings.

The EDGAR website is open on business days (Monday through Friday) from 8:00 a.m. to 10:00 p.m. Eastern time. Filings received during open hours will be receive a same-day filing date and will be available to the public on the day of filing.

No special software is needed to file through the SEC EDGAR website, but most available stock administration programs will create a reduced-content XML of the Forms, which can be uploaded to EDGAR. Whether filed directly or uploaded, write down the accession number (used to verify the submission) provided after the transmission has been submitted. You will also receive email confirmation of the filing from the SEC.

EDGAR Access Codes
Every company and insider will have a unique set of EDGAR access codes. As an individual with responsibility for filing with the SEC, it's a good idea for you to have your own EDGAR access codes, but you can also sign in to EDGAR with a company CIK and password.

CIK: Central Index Key. Public number used to uniquely identify companies and individuals filing reports with the SEC. Assigned by the SEC at the time of initial application, CIKs can be looked up on the SEC's website.
CCC: CIK Confirmation Code. Used in conjunction with the CIK to confirm filing authorization.
Password: Used to log onto the EDGAR system, submit filings, and change CCC. Updated annually.
PMAC: Password Modification Authorization Code. Allows you to change your password.
Passphrase: Used to create or change a CCC, Password, or PMAC. Not necessary for routine filings, as it is used only to generate a new access code in the absence of the old ones.

Remember, every insider has one unique set of EDGAR access codes, so it is important to ask them if they already have EDGAR access codes before requesting a new set.

Obtaining Access Codes
If you have your own CIK and password, you can use them to file forms as a filing agent for any/all insiders. If you file forms using insider codes, you need to have a separate set of codes for each insider. And if you do not have your own codes, don't have the insider's codes, but need to file immediately to meet a deadline, you can always try filing with the company's codes to avoid blatant noncompliance.

If an insider already has codes, you'll need to maintain contact with any/all other companies for which the insider has filing responsibility to determine who will be responsible for managing that insider's EDGAR access codes. And if you request codes for an insider, be sure to communicate the codes to that insider so that they can transmit the codes and your contact information in the event that they become reporting individuals for some other company.

Form ID is used to apply for EDGAR access codes for insiders or filers who do not already have access codes. This form can be downloaded from the SEC website. Form ID must be filed electronically via EDGAR, and a notarized copy with manual signature must be filed in paper by fax within two business days before or after electronic filing. Response and instructions are received by email.

Once you have your CIK and Password, you can log into EDGAR. At first use of a CIK on EDGAR, you will be required to create a Passphrase, using the PMAC.

Filing via EDGAR
Follow the directions provided online. If you need assistance, call one of the numbers provided above.

Post-Filing
All Section 16 reports must be posted on company websites by the end of the business day after filing, so be sure your IT department is aware of your timeline. You can either post the reports themselves or a link directly to only and specifically the Section 16 reports on the SEC website.

Section 16 Officer—Initial Information Capture

Fill in the information you have in your records and give this form to each Section 16 Officer upon election for verification, clarification, completion, and signature. Update, print, and ask for verification every time information changes are received.

1. What is the full name of this Section 16 officer?
2. If different, the exact name that this person uses for EDGAR filing purposes?
3. On what date was this person born?
4. What is this person's taxpayer ID number/Social Security number?
5. On what date was this person hired, or on what date did this person's service with the company commence?
    i) ☐ **Attach copy of Section 16 designation (from board minutes).**
6. What is this person's address of record?
7. Does this person have another address? What is it?
8. What are this person's contact phone number(s)?
9. What is this person's e-mail address? Business/personal?
10. To what tax authority does this person report (what is the state of residence for tax purposes)?
11. What is this person's withholding obligation?
12. Who is this person's broker? Make sure you receive all contact information.
13. Does the company have a power of attorney on file for this person? Who holds it?
    i) ☐ **Attach copy of power of attorney.**
14. What is the insider's EDGAR CIK (Central Index Key)?
15. What is the insider's EDGAR CCC (CIK Confirmation Code)?
16. What is the insider's EDGAR Password?
17. What is the insider's EDGAR PMAC (Password Modification Access Code)?
18. What is the insider's EDGAR Passphrase?
19. Especially if this insider has reporting responsibility with other companies, who manages their EDGAR access codes? Is it you or someone else at this company? Someone at another company?
20. Are there any other companies for which this person must report under Section 16?

**If your company has a preclearance policy for sale of company stock by Section 16 officers, attach it and replace "I hereby certify that the information above is correct to the best of my knowledge." with "I hereby certify that the information above is correct to the best of my knowledge and that I have read and agree to abide by the terms of the attached preclearance policy for sale of company stock." or some other phraseology that your legal counsel approves. With your legal department's blessing, you can also add a clause agreeing to report all trades to you within a stated period following the trade.

Section 16 Officer—Initial Information Capture

1. Full name: _____
2. Name as used for EDGAR filings (if different): _____
3. Date of birth: _____
4. TIN/SSN: _____
5. Date of hire/date of commencement of service: _____
6. Address of record: _____
7. Additional address: _____
8. Phone number/s: _____
9. E-mail address: _____
10. Tax authority: _____
11. Withholding obligation: _____
12. Broker (and contact info): _____
13. Power of attorney on file? Y/N   If yes, designee _____
14. EDGAR CIK: _____
15. EDGAR CCC: _____
16. EDGAR Password: _____
17. EDGAR PMAC: _____
18. EDGAR Passphrase: _____
19. EDGAR access code manager: _____
20. Other companies with which a Section 16 reporting relationship is maintained:
    Company: _____ Contact: _____
    Company: _____ Contact: _____
    Company: _____ Contact: _____

I hereby certify that the information above is correct to the best of my knowledge.

Signed: _____

Date: _____

Section 16 Officer—Stock Holdings

This memorandum (D&O Questionnaire) should be completed and distributed in advance of any reports requiring Section 16 Officer stock holdings.

Date: *(date of distribution)*

To: *(Section 16 Officer)*

From: *(Company's General Counsel/Section 16 Forms Preparer)*

In order to prepare _____*(enter the name of the form to be filed)*_____, please indicate/confirm below *(choose one of the options—for indicate below, leave the second column blank; for confirm below, enter the numbers you have on file)* the exact number of shares of common stock and securities convertible into common stock of __*(Company Name)*____ you own as of ____*(date of triggering event/period end date)*_____. Please complete this memorandum and return it to ___*(Section 16 forms preparer)*_____ as soon as possible so that the _____*(form to be filed)*_____ can be completed and filed no later than _____*(date form is required to be filed)*_____.

Table:

As of *(date of last submission for persons who have previously reported holdings to you—this column may be deleted for Form 3 filings- and complete the column with the figures you have on file)*

As of *(date of triggering event/period end date—leave this column blank or complete as indicated above)*:

A-E. As explained.

F. Stock options held: track details as shown.

    ISO/NSO Grant date: _____ Options Granted: _____ Vesting: _____

G. Restricted stock awards: track details as shown.

    Award date: _____ Shares Granted: _____ Vesting/Lapse: _____

H. As explained (insert Company Name where indicated).

Section 16 Officer—Stock Holdings

Date: _____

To: _____

From: _____

In order to prepare _____, please indicate/confirm below the exact number of shares of common stock and securities convertible into common stock of _____ you own as of _____. Please complete this memorandum and return it to _____ as soon as possible so that the _____ can be completed and filed no later than _____.

Form of Ownership	As of _____:	As of _____:
A. Shares held directly (includes shares registered in your name, shares held in street name for your account, and shares in dividend reinvestment plans).		
B. Shares held indirectly (by spouse, minor children, custodial accounts, relatives sharing your home, etc.).		
C. Shares held by you as a trustee. Co-Trustee(s): _____ Beneficiaries: _____		
D. Shares owned directly by others, over which you share voting power and/or investment power. This may include shares held by a partnership of which you are a partner, an estate of which you are a beneficiary, or a corporation or other organization that you control.		
E. Shares held directly by anyone else under any arrangements not mentioned above from which you receive benefits of ownership.		
F. Stock options held.		
G. Restricted stock awards.		
H. Puts, calls, warrants, and other rights to acquire _____ stock.		

Beneficial ownership is presumed disclaimed unless otherwise indicated.

I hereby certify that the information above is correct to the best of my knowledge.

Signature: _____ Date: _____

Chapter 5: Contacts & Meetings

Establishing and maintaining good communication lines and data flows is a lot harder than it seems. It's so easy to get caught up in what needs to be done that you don't always get a chance to step back to make sure that everyone's being taken care of in the way they need to be.

First of all, you need to have some information clearly posted in your office so that if you're out and a time-sensitive situation comes up, it's easy to figure out who to call. *"Designated Contacts"* can be posted in multiple places to help you and everyone else at the company quickly identify where to route inquiries. Some address inquiries that will be coming into the company (e.g., media inquiries), some have to do with employee inquiries (e.g., broker), and some are to expedite other departments redirection (e.g., outsource firms). It really helps to have designated point people so that messages can be consistent and there's no confusion about who's handling what. In addition, *"Stock Administration Team"* will contain many of the same contacts as above, but provides more detail and is really meant for just your team.

You probably already have a calendar, but the basic grid *"Calendar"* is provided because so few people step back to look at the year's flow all at once. If you keep an electronic calendar, all the better—just remember to actually print out an annual look so you can see your workload concentrations. You'd hate to have your blackout window lift during the week your outsource administrator is offline for annual maintenance, or to schedule a series of educational workshops for your employees offsite during the week leading up to a board meeting . . .

That said, though, educating your employees about how their equity ownership works and why that's a good thing can make a huge difference in your corporate culture. How can people value something they don't understand? And why give people something that they don't think is a benefit to them? *"Equity Education"* helps you track the various educational events you offer to the different groups and departments you come in contact with. You may also use *"Meeting Details"* to take a more meticulous look at the events you're planning. It helps to track administrivia, demand, and attendance patterns for future years as you go through the same cycle of meetings again.

And your shareholders do own the company, so you'll need to provide a lot of financial information annually so you can produce your annual report and proxy statement. The *"Annual Meeting"* template will need to be tweaked for your company, but it's here to get you used to writing down your timeline to let other people know what needs to be done when as well as to help other people step in if needed.

Equity Compensation Contacts

This is essential to have posted by anyone who answers the phone, as well as every member of your team. Be sure to distribute for replacement of all copies when updating information.

What person at your company is the primary point of contact for each of these people/groups? Who receives/ writes/ sends/ signs communications to each of these people/groups? (include phone number/ extension)
  i) Especially if it's you, who's the backup if the first point of contact is unavailable?

a) Who sends out communications to your employees about changes to the plan? Blackout windows?

b) Who handles compliance, insider trading, or pre-clearance issues?

c) Who sends out communications to your shareholders? If a shareholder calls with a question, whom do they talk to?

d) Who handles investor relations?

e) If someone calls in from a newspaper, whom do you have them talk to?

f) Who handles the transfer agent relationship? If your contact at the transfer agent quits unexpectedly and their replacement calls the switchboard, whom should they connect her to?

g) Who handles the broker relationship? If your contact at the broker quits unexpectedly and their replacement calls the switchboard, or if an outside broker calls with questions, whom should they connect her to?

h) Who provides the auditors with any information they request?

i) Who provides accounting with any information requested or required?

j) Who provides payroll with any information requested or required?

k) Who provides tax information as needed? Who answers questions about taxes?

l) If you outsource your stock administration, who handles that relationship?

m) Any others not mentioned above?

n) Any others not mentioned above?

Equity Compensation Contacts

a) Employee communications: _____

    i) Backup: _____

b) Compliance: _____

    i) Backup: _____

c) Shareholder communications: _____

    i) Backup: _____

d) Investor communications: _____

    i) Backup: _____

e) Media inquiries on equity compensation: _____

    i) Backup: _____

f) Transfer Agent: _____

    i) Backup: _____

g) Broker: _____

    i) Backup: _____

h) Auditor: _____

    i) Backup: _____

i) Accounting: _____

    i) Backup: _____

j) Payroll: _____

    i) Backup: _____

k) Taxes: _____

    i) Backup: _____

l) Stock administration outsource firm: _____

    i) Backup: _____

m) _____

    i) Backup: _____

n) _____

    i) Backup: _____

Last updated _____

Stock Administration Team

This grid is great to hang on your wall for quick reference, as well as to distribute to your entire group. This isn't just for you, but for anyone who needs to fill in for you or handle emergencies when you're not around. Yes, you may have this all electronically already, in which case you might just want to print what you have and post it, but in any case, make this information visible for someone who might not be able to get into your computer.

Function: What function does this person serve in the broad overview of your stock administration? What is the main purpose of your contact with them? Is this the person in accounting who handles payroll issues or capitalization tables? For example:

> INTERNAL (INT): Payroll, HR-benefits, HR-recruiting, legal counsel, finance, mailings, compliance officer, blackout periods, transfer agent, media, etc.

> EXTERNAL (EXT): Broker, transfer agent, legal counsel, tax accountant, auditors, outside stock administrator, printer, etc.

Comments: What hours/days is this person in the office? What time zone does she/he work in? What primary functions does she/he handle?

Name: How does this person prefer to be addressed?

Direct dial: Phone number—with extension if necessary.

E-mail: E-mail address.

Other phone: Mobile phone? Pager? Alternate phone?

Company/department: What company does this person work for? If it's the same company as you, what department are they in (INT-Accounting)?

Company phone: Is there a main line for the company? Is there a toll-free number? A number for this company you give out to your employees?

Assistant/Backup: Does this person have an assistant? Is there someone to contact if this person is out of the office and you need an immediate response?

Fax: Fax number.

Stock Administration Team

Function	Comments		Other Phone
Name	Direct Dial	Email	
Company/Department	Company Phone	Assistant/Backup	Fax
F	C		
N	DD	E	OP
C/D	CP	A/B	F
F	C		
N	DD	E	OP
C/D	CP	A/B	F
F	C		
N	DD	E	OP
C/D	CP	A/B	F
F	C		
N	DD	E	OP
C/D	CP	A/B	F
F	C		
N	DD	E	OP
C/D	CP	A/B	F
F	C		
N	DD	E	OP
C/D	CP	A/B	F

Calendar

If you use an electronic calendar, this might not be anything new. It is important, though, to take the time to look at the big picture yearly calendar every so often.

At the beginning of the year, take the time to enter all the planning items you know in the appropriate dates—equity education meetings, quarter and year end activities, blackout periods, annual meeting, reporting deadlines, etc. Include any dates that might impact your planning or activities—weekends/ holidays/ vendor holidays, etc. Don't forget to enter in the NCEO and NASPP annual conferences, as well as chapter meetings and any workshops or seminars you'll be attending to maintain your CEP!

Some entries, such as the "6039 reports" entry shown, you'll use to alert you to mandatory filing or mailing deadlines so that you can plan accordingly; for example, you might want to schedule the report run for the week or two weeks before so that they can be checked and mailed on time.

By planning carefully, you can avoid scheduling conflicts that would detract from your ability to function as efficiently or smoothly as desired; e.g., inadvertently scheduling a series of informational meetings for the week before your proxy information is due.

You can distribute this completed grid to the management team at your company, and to the heads of any other departments, to help with interdepartmental scheduling. Often, something as easy as providing your timelines to other people helps them understand why you need things by certain dates and to get information to you in a more timely fashion.

Calendar Year

	January	February	March	April	May	June	July	August	September	October	November	December
1												
2												
3												
4												
5												
6												
7												
8												
9												
10												
11												
12												
13												
14												
15												
16												
17												
18												
19												
20												
21												
22												
23												
24												
25												
26												
27												
28												
29												
30												
31	6039 reports											

Equity Education

Take the time to make sure everyone understands what's going on with equity compensation. It not only saves you the time involved with answering tons of individual (and often duplicative) inquiries, but often improves both morale and productivity as well!

- Be sure to keep track of the education provided by filing a packet for each meeting held that includes the date, agenda, list of attendees, and handouts provided.
- Keep a few extra agenda/handout packets on hand so you can give them to anyone who missed the meeting but wants the resources.
- Don't cover too many topics at once in a meeting, but make multiple meetings/topics available to present information in digestible chunks.
- Make sure your meeting times and places are accessible to all employees—swing and night shift employees need information too!
- Also consider holding sets of "office hours" in public areas such as break rooms or lunch rooms to increase your availability to answer employee questions.
- Focus on how the plan features support corporate and participant goals.
- Hold at least one meeting annually for everyone who handles any part of the equity administration function to make sure you all have the same basic information down.

Suggested topics for stock education:

Employees
- How equity compensation works, plan basics, where information resides on the intranet/internet, whom to contact for what, calendar/timing issues, taxation questions and references.
- Will you conduct regularly scheduled informational meetings for new hires? When? Will you meet individually with each new hire or with a group of new hires all at once? Will you hold new hire meetings on a regular schedule or as hires are made?
- How often will you hold informational meetings for your optionees/grantees? Annually? Quarterly? Monthly? Will you schedule meetings to correspond with vesting dates? Before significant events?
- Will you hold any year-end meetings (usually November or December) to help get your employees started thinking about year-end tax planning and related issues?
- What outside experts can you bring in to help with financial planning or other issues?

Human Resources
- How equity compensation works, plan basics, mechanics and timeline of grant/option process, data flows, communication strategies and approaches, corporate policies on plan communication, broker information.

Recruiting
- General terms and conditions of plan, mechanics and timeline of grant/option process, parameters of equity compensation discussions with prospective employees, comparison with other companies' plans, and, of course, the benefits of yours!

Finance
- Accounting and tax implications of plan variables for both company and employees, reporting requirements, data flows.

Payroll
- Reporting for W-2/1099 purposes, ESPP deduction policies, and schedules.

Legal
- Review of or creation process for materials you plan to distribute, including insider trading policy education plan, compliance issues.

Management team
- How equity compensation works, plan basics, limitations on discussions with prospective employees, communication policies, insider trading policies, 10b5-1 plans, pre-clearance policy.

Executive team
- How stock options work, plan basics, limitations on discussions with prospective employees, communication policies, insider trading policies, pre-clearance policy, Section 16 filings and penalties for delinquent filings, reporting requirements and indirect holdings, 10b5-1 plans, Sarbanes-Oxley issues, Section 162(m) issues.

Board of directors
- Plan basics, insider trading policies, pre-clearance policy, Section 16 filings and penalties for delinquent filings, reporting requirements and indirect holdings, 10b5-1 plans, Sarbanes-Oxley issues.

Shareholder/Investor Relations
- Plan basics, how to explain plans to shareholders/investors, presentations to analysts and financial press, Sarbanes-Oxley issues.

Meeting Details

1. When will this meeting be held—during business hours or not? Have you checked for any date conflicts (software releases, benefits enrollment, etc.)?
    a. When did you send the meeting announcement or post the meeting on your intranet? Reminders?
2. What topic(s) will be covered? (e.g.; new hire info, taxes, how to work with a brokerage, etc.)
3. Where will the meeting be held? If at an outside location, have you provided the attendees with directions, maps, and parking information?
    a. Under what name is the space reserved? What block of time is the space reserved for—when can you arrive for setup?
    b. Who is your contact for the reservation?
4. Do you provide the information and speak yourself or do you plan the meetings with your broker, finance department, or legal counsel? Do you bring in an outside tax accountant or attorney? Who will the primary speaker(s) be?
    a. Be sure to confirm the date with your speaker both before announcing the meeting and one week before the meeting.
    b. Confirm the topic to be discussed, as well as the target audience
    c. Will the speaker send you an electronic version of the presentation for your files or to pre-load at the meeting space?
    d. Will the speaker expect you to produce handouts or will they bring them with them?
5. Will any special equipment be necessary—e.g.; computer, monitor, projector, projection screen, microphone(s), podium, overhead projector, etc.?
    a. Ensure that the equipment you need will be available, then confirm the day before the meeting.
    b. Who is your contact for the equipment?
6. Will you be distributing information to attendees? Who will prepare them?
    a. What is the title of the electronic document(s)? (this is especially important to write down in case someone else needs to take over from you)
    b. Have you saved it to disk to file with the meeting information?
    c. Don't forget to file a copy.
7. Will you be providing refreshments to attendees? Is this a brown bag lunch or a company-sponsored lunch? Milk and cookies?
    a. Note vendor contact information.
8. How many people do you expect to have there?
    a. (*after the meeting*) How many people attended?

Meeting Details

1. Date/time: _____
   a) Meeting announcement: _____ Reminder: _____
2. Topic: _____
3. Location: _____
   a) Space reservation information: _____
   b) Space contact information: _____
4. Speaker(s): _____
   a) Date confirmed: _____
   b) Topic confirmed: _____
   c) Sending you electronic copy of presentation? Y/N
   d) Handouts? Y/N Prepared by: _____
5. Equipment needed: _____
   a) Confirmed availability? Y/N Confirmed the day before the meeting? Y/N
   b) Contact information: _____
6. Handouts? Y/N Prepared by?: _____
   a) Title of electronic document/s: _____
   b) Disk attached for file? Y/N
   c) Copy attached for file? Y/N
7. Refreshments provided: _____
   a) Contact/vendor information: _____
8. Number of attendees anticipated: _____
   a) Number of people actually there: _____

Annual Meeting

Date/Time: _____
Location: _____

Target Date   Actual Date

_____ _____ Begin drafting Proxy Statement, Proxy Card and D&O Questionnaires
(4 months prior)

_____ _____ Announce Annual Meeting date, record dates
(3 months prior)

_____ _____ Notify transfer agent and proxy solicitor of annual meeting and record dates.

_____ _____ Canvass Brokers and other Nominees
    (must be at least 20 business days prior to record date)

_____ _____ Due date for return of D&O Questionnaires

_____ _____ RECORD DATE
(2 months prior)

_____ _____ File proxy statement

_____ _____ Authorize Printer to begin printing of proxy statement.

_____ _____ PROXY MAIL DATE
(7 weeks prior)

_____ _____ Prepare meeting materials—agenda, script, ballots, etc.
(5 weeks prior)

_____ _____ Prepare list of shareholders entitled to vote at meeting
(2 weeks prior)

_____ _____ ANNUAL MEETING

Chapter 6: Regular Updates

Every year certain things need to happen on schedule. You need to use some form of this *"Basic Period-End Checklist"* for every major calendar and fiscal period end. This is definitely a list that you should expand with other things you do at your company; the items listed are simply to give you a base and format for preparation. You can use this to assign tasks (keep a copy for yourself) or to keep track of what you need to do as it gets done.

This might go on your checklist, or you may want to schedule it for a less hectic time, but *"Stock Plan Security and Data Retention"* is a questionnaire you should complete at least annually. If you use a third-party administrator, ask these questions of them as well. Just don't put this off for too long—it's like disability insurance in that so long as your data's healthy and moving along well it can be hard to justify putting in the annual premium, but if anything goes wrong, that time was *so* worth it.

Likewise, you don't want to suddenly realize that your stock plan expires tomorrow, with a long list of new hire grants ready to go to the compensation committee, two months before the next board meeting. Or worse yet, that it's already expired! You should complete the *"Stock Plan Maintenance"* questionnaire annually, for every stock plan your company maintains, and follow up in any area that seems loose. It's worth the time.

Basic Period-End Checklist

Period Start Date: _____ **Period End Date:** _____

Assigned to: _____

Target Date	Date Done	
Period End	_____	Back up stock plan database (at least quarterly if not more often).
P- End +1	_____	Back up stock plan database AGAIN.
_____	_____	Reconcile all plan balances (monthly).
_____	_____	Ensure that all data for the period has been entered and that any errors have been corrected and/or documented (monthly).
_____	_____	Verify with Human Resources that all new hires, terminations, leaves, deaths, and status changes—both employee and consultant—have been input into stock plan database (monthly).
_____	_____	Reconcile plan reserves and cap table with Transfer Agent (monthly).
_____	_____	Provide Finance with all stock option (ESPP/ISO/NSO) reports showing reportable income, tax credits, and taxes withheld for W-2/1099 inclusion (monthly/quarterly).
_____	_____	Update capitalization table (quarterly).
_____	_____	Send notice of blackout period to all affected persons (quarterly).
_____	_____	Blackout period starts: block insider accounts if necessary (quarterly).
_____	_____	Verify that all 83(b) elections made have been properly reported as income (quarterly).
_____	_____	Verify tax rates and limits (Social Security, Medicare, state taxes)—update any that have changed. (calendar year-end)
_____	_____	Distribute 6039 statements (Jan 31 deadline).
_____	_____	Zero out all YTD figures, including taxes paid. (year-end)
_____	_____	Verify that no employee has exceeded the ESPP $25,000 limit prior to year-end purchase. (year-end)
_____	_____	Update all plan reserves. (year-end)
_____	_____	Distribute ISO/ESPP disqualifying disposition statements. (year-end)
_____	_____	Prepare & distribute D&O ?aires for Proxy & Forms 5. (year-end)
_____	_____	Schedule equity education meetings and distribute schedule. (annual)
_____	_____	Verify EDGAR password expirations and change if necessary. (annual)
_____	_____	Verify Insider Trading & Watch lists with Legal/Compliance. (annual)
_____	_____	Verify termination dates of all plans. (annual)
_____	_____	Verify plan reserves to ensure that share balances in all plans will cover anticipated distributions in the coming year. (annual)

Stock Plan Security and Data Retention

1. Where is your physical stock plan information stored? _____
2. Are the file cabinets locked when not in use? Y/N
3. Who has access to the room? _____ Custodial Staff? Y/N
4. Who has access to the files? _____
5. How long are physical records kept? _____
6. Who is in charge of purging records? _____

7. What computer program(s) do you use to track equity? _____
8. Where is your electronic stock plan information stored? _____
9. Who has the authority to grant/deny access privileges? _____
   - Who has add/change/delete access? _____ IT Staff? Y/N
   - Who has read-only access? _____ IT Staff? Y/N
   - Who is the contact to change access privileges? _____
10. Is remote access of stock plan information allowed? Y/N
    - If yes, to whom? _____
    - Are all remote access ports secure? _____
11. How often are regular backups performed? _____
    - Who performs the backups? _____
    - Where are the backup files stored? _____
12. Do you also perform backups after high activity periods? Y/N
    - If yes, who performs those backups? _____
    - Where are those files stored? _____
13. Do you have a disaster recovery plan in place? Y/N
    - If yes, attach a copy.

Stock Plan Maintenance

1. What is the name of the plan being assessed? _____
2. On what date is this assessment being made? _____
3. Does this plan meet requirements for applicable treatment/exemptions in the following areas? (If yes, provide detail.)
    a. Tax   Y/N _____
    b. Securities Y/N _____
    c. Accounting Y/N _____
4. Are the shares subject to this plan registered with the SEC? Y/N _____
5. When does this plan expire? _____
6. If the plan is set to expire within the next two years, have provisions been made for either an extension of the plan or for a new plan to be drafted/approved? Y/N _____
7. How many shares are available for issuance? _____
8. Are the shares available for issuance adequate for demand? Y/N _____
9. If not, have provisions been made to ensure that adequate shares will be available when required? Y/N _____
10. Have there been any incidents since the last assessment where a situation was not addressed or a definition was not clear? Y/N
    a. If yes, write a detailed description of the incident along with the solution that was reached and file with the plan.
11. Attach a summary of the options/shares subject to this plan with reconciliations if applicable.

Chapter 7: Glossapedia

$1 Million Cap
Under Internal Revenue Code Section 162(m), the maximum amount of non-incentive-based executive compensation a company may take as a tax deduction.

$100,000 Rule
Under Internal Revenue Code Section 422(d), no more than $100,000 in aggregate fair market value of incentive stock options granted to any one person may become first exercisable in any calendar year; any options granted past this limit are automatically disqualified from statutory option treatment. If the company fails to properly designate ISO and NSO stock, the first $100,000 (based on value at grant) of stock issued is ISO stock and the remainder is NSO stock.

Options that are not ISOs at grant do not apply to this limit. Options are generally taken into account in the order in which they are granted. If the option loses ISO status due to cancellation, modification, or transfer prior to the year in which it first becomes exercisable, it is disregarded for the year in which it first becomes exercisable. If the option is canceled, modified, or transferred in any other situation, it must still be taken into account in the year in which it would otherwise have first become exercisable.

6 + 1
See "Option Exchange."

10% Owner
(1) For tax purposes, any person who owns stock representing 10% or more of the total combined voting power of all classes of stock of the company. Incentive stock options granted to 10% owners must (a) have an exercise price of at least 110% of the fair market value on the date of grant, and (b) have a term of no more than five years.

(2) For Section 16 purposes, the beneficial owner of more than 10% of a class of equity securities of a public company.

10b5-1
See "Rule 10b5-1."

10b5-1 Plan
Program that allows the buying or selling of company stock at predetermined intervals and amounts by insiders regardless of possession of confidential information.

83(b) Election
See "Section 83(b) Election."

423 Plan
See "Internal Revenue Code, Section 423."

1933 Act
See "Securities Act of 1933."

1934 Act
See "Securities Exchange Act of 1934."

Abandoned Property
See "Escheatment."

Accelerated Vesting
Situation in which the rate at which a stock option vests is increased, often in a cliff vesting fashion. Accelerated vesting is generally the result of either performance goals being met or a corporate transaction taking place.

Accounting Principles Board (APB)
Established by the American Institute of Certified Public Accountants to develop and establish GAAP by issuing opinions and decisions. Preceded by the Committee on Accounting Procedure of the American Institute of Certified Public Accountants (1936-1959) and succeeded by the Financial Accounting Standards Board (FASB) in 1973. See "APB 25."

Accredited Investor
Investors meeting a minimum level of investment sophistication or who show wealth or income characteristics such as a net worth of more than $1 million. Accredited investors are permitted to participate in private placements and unregistered securities. See "Private Placement."

Accrued Interest
Interest that has been earned but not yet paid.

Acquisition
The purchase of a company by another entity. An acquisition is a change in control event that often triggers changes in vesting schedules as described in stock plan documents.

Additional Paid-In Capital (APIC)
Accounting term for the comparison of equity-related deferred tax assets with the actual tax deduction taken. At the time of the event that results in a corporate tax deduction, any amount of tax deduction that exceeds the DTA already recorded is added to the APIC pool. If the DTA exceeds the actual tax deduction, any amounts residing in the existing APIC pool may be used to offset the DTA, but if the APIC pool cannot cover the difference, any amount remaining becomes a tax expense recognized in the same period as the tax deduction.

Additive SAR
Stock appreciation right that can be exercised simultaneously with a stock option exercise to provide cash to offset taxes due on the option exercised.

Administrator
See "Stock Administrator," "Plan Administrator."

Affiliate
Rule 144 term for a control person (director, executive officer, etc.) of a company. Affiliates are subject to limitations on timing and volume of sale of unregistered stock.

Alternative Minimum Tax (AMT)

The AMT requires taxpayers to make an alternate income tax calculation by not excluding certain deductions and exclusions they are entitled to in their regular income tax calculation, then comparing that amount with their regular income tax. AMT is calculated on IRS Form 6251 and entered as a line item on IRS Form 1040.

The exercise of an ISO is a "tax preference item" requiring the AMT calculation unless the ISO was vested at exercise and an 83(b) form has been filed. The spread on an ISO is among the items that must be included in the AMT calculation.

There is no way to determine what amount, if any, will be owed under the AMT until both regular income tax and AMT calculations are complete. If you exercise a significant value in options, though, it would be wise to consult a tax professional at the time of exercise to estimate how much money should be put aside for potential tax liability. If the AMT rate is higher than the normal tax rate, AMT is due, but the amount paid that exceeds what would have been paid under the regular income tax calculation can be used as a credit in future years when the AMT would provide a tax liability lower than regular income tax.

AMT tax basis is the amount paid plus the AMT adjustment made. This means that when an employee has to pay an AMT adjustment on shares acquired under an ISO and not sold by the end of the tax year, the tax basis for future AMT calculations is increased by the amount of AMT paid at exercise of the ISO shares; for calculating the gain for ordinary income tax purposes, the basis remains the amount the employee had to pay to exercise the option.

American Institute of Certified Public Accountants (AICPA)

Membership organization for certified public accountants.

American Jobs Creation Act of 2004 (AJCA)

Signed into law on October 22, 2004, Section 885 of the American Jobs Creation Act of 2004 (AJCA) most notably creates new Section 409A of the Internal Revenue Code. Under the Act, vested nonqualified deferred compensation becomes taxable on a current basis unless certain requirements are met.

IRC Section 409A is effective in regard to awards granted or vested after December 31, 2004. Internal Revenue Service Notice 2005-1 "Transition Guidance on Section 409A" was published on January 10, 2005 to provide clarification.

In addition, Section 251 of the AJCA exempts ISO and 423 plan ESPP stock from withholding for FICA, FUTA, and applicable federal, state, and local tax, and Section 904 imposes a 35% withholding rate on income recognized from stock option exercise, restricted stock vesting, restricted unit and phantom stock release, bonuses, and other supplemental wage payments in excess of $1 million.

See "Internal Revenue Code, Section 409A."

American Stock Exchange (AMEX)

Second-largest organized U.S. stock exchange. It is generally considered to have less stringent listing requirements than the New York Stock Exchange, and trades mostly in securities of small to medium sized corporations. The AMEX competes with the NYSE and NASDAQ to list companies' securities for trading. For trading schedules, go to *www.amex.com*, then navigate to At the AMEX/About the AMEX/Holiday Calendar. See "Securities Exchange," "Self-Regulatory Organization."

APIC
See "Additional Paid-In Capital."

AMEX
See "American Stock Exchange."

Amortization
(1) Gradual extinguishment of a debt, generally through a systematic payment plan that applies payments to both principal and interest in a predetermined ratio; (2) writing off of an intangible asset investment over the projected life of the asset.

Amount Realized
Tax concept representing the difference between the amount paid for property and the amount received upon sale or exchange of the property—also called gain or profit.

AMT
See "Alternative Minimum Tax."

Annual Meeting
Once-a-year meeting of the directors, officers, and shareholders of a corporation to communicate the business results for the preceding fiscal year, plans for the future, and any material changes in management or to previously communicated plans. Voting for election of directors or on corporate matters may be done either in person or by proxy.

In advance of the Annual Meeting, mailings must be sent to all shareholders of record as of a designated record date and meeting materials must be prepared. *See Chapter 5: Annual Meeting.*

Annual Report to Shareholders
Report sent annually, generally around the time of the annual meeting, used to disclose corporate information to shareholders; usually includes an opening letter from the chief executive officer, financial data, results of continuing operations, market segment information, new product plans, subsidiary activities, and research and development activities on future programs.

Anti-Dilution Adjustment
Adjustment made to the terms, conditions, and/or price of a security to maintain value in response to a change in capital structure of the corporation.

APB
See "Accounting Principles Board."

APB 25
Accounting Principles Board Opinion No. 25, "Accounting for Stock Issued to Employees," issued in 1972. Used in parallel with FAS 123, then superseded by FAS 123R in 2004. Established

the intrinsic value method of accounting for stock options. *See Chapter 2: Accounting Overview: APB Opinion 25.*

Asset
As an accounting term, something of value that is owned and can be listed on the balance sheet.

Attestation
Affidavit or declaration of share ownership by which the surrender of a physical stock certificate can be circumnavigated.

Audit
Review of a company's financial records, either as a regularly scheduled annual audit, or under investigation by an interested party or agency.

Auditors
Financial personnel charged with performing an audit.

Authorized but Unissued
See "Shares Authorized but Unissued."

Automatic Low Offering Period
ESPP offering period that automatically terminates as of any exercise date on which the FMV of the stock being purchased is lower than the FMV of the stock on the date of grant.

Available for Grant
Shares of securities authorized for issuance under a corporation's stock plan, less the number of shares that have already been granted, plus any canceled shares added back to the plan, and plus any shares added to the plan for issuance.

Bankruptcy
The legally declared inability of an individual or organization to pay their creditors, bankruptcy allows the debtor to resolve his debts and be discharged of most financial obligations through the division of his assets among his creditors even if the debts have not been paid in full. There are two types of bankruptcy proceedings: liquidation under Chapter 7, and rehabilitation under Chapters 11, 12, and 13. The transfer of an ISO share under title 11 or any other similar insolvency proceeding is not considered a disqualifying disposition of the ISO stock.

Bargain Element
See "Spread."

Basis
The amount paid for stock plus any compensation income reported.

Bear Market
Weak securities market characterized by declining prices.

Beneficial Owner
For securities purposes, any person or entity who controls voting and/or investment power in a security whether held in one name or many (e.g., a shareholder may beneficially own shares in the names of her spouse and children, as well as her own).

Beneficial Ownership
The right to economic benefit from a transaction in securities, whether or not the beneficial owner is the owner of record of the securities in question. See "Indirect Ownership."

Bid-and-Asked Quotation
Stock price quoted as a range from the "bid," the highest price offered, to the "asked," the lowest price someone will accept, at any given time.

Binomial Option Pricing Model
Mathematical formula used to determine the value of a stock option by computing a lattice, or tree, of possible outcomes. A binomial model assumes two possible outcomes from any point in the lattice.

Black-Scholes Option Pricing Model
Nobel prize-winning mathematical formula developed by Fischer Black and Myron Scholes to value options traded on European commodity exchanges, commonly applied in a modified form to the valuation of employee stock options.

There are six required variables used in calculating fair value: (1) exercise price; (2) current market price of underlying stock; (3) expected life of the option; (4) expected dividends on the underlying stock; (5) expected interest rate on risk-free securities during the expected life of the option; and (6) the expected volatility of underlying stock (not applicable for nonpublic companies).

Blackout Period
Period during which the securities of a corporation cannot be traded by Section 16 insiders or holders of material nonpublic information about the company and its affairs: the converse of an open window. Blackout periods generally bracket the release of annual or quarterly financial results, but can occur any time financial or material information about the company is released. Blackout periods are established by the company, generally by the compliance officer, and communicated in advance to any affected parties. *See Chapter 4: Section 16 Filings: Blackout Periods.*

Blanket Opinion
Legal opinion issued by corporate counsel after registration statements have been filed and approved, providing service providers such as brokers and transfer agents the information they need to allow the transfer of legended stock certificates and previously restricted securities.

Block
Large amount of securities, generally a minimum of either 10,000 shares or $200,000 in value.

Blue Chip Stock
Common stock issued by a financially strong, stable company with a good history of dividend payments, offering a low-risk investment.

Blue Sky Laws
Originally taken from a Supreme Court opinion referencing "speculative schemes which have no more basis than so many feet of blue sky," "blue sky laws" is the common term for state statutes regulating the offer and sale of securities as well as the registration and reporting requirements for broker-dealers, investment brokers, and investment advisors within a state's jurisdiction.

Blue Sky Law Reporter
Produced by CCH, a compilation of all Blue Sky statutes, regulations, and summaries of cases.

Board of Directors
A group of people elected by a corporation's shareholders to control or govern the affairs of the corporation. The board is generally comprised of multiple committees that play an oversight role over different areas of the organization, such as compensation, audit, and finance.

Boilerplate
Term for a generic base document, to be customized as needed for the task at hand.

Bond
Formal certificate of indebtedness issued by a corporation as security for a loan.

Book Entry
The tracking of shares by a transfer agent without the issuance of a physical certificate.

Book Value
Amount by which a company's assets exceed its liabilities, also called net worth or shareholders' equity, divided by the number of shares of stock outstanding. If the company has issued preferred stock, the value of the preferred stock must be deducted from shareholders' equity to determine the book value of the common stock.

Books
Financial records of a company; currently companies keep one set of books for financial accounting and one set of books for tax filing.

Broad-Based Stock Plan
Stock plan designed for the purpose of granting stock at all levels of a company. Usually a stock plan whereby 50% or more of the employees of the company receive grants, often a stock plan where substantially all employees are eligible to participate regardless of actual participation rates.

Broker/Brokerage Firm
Individual or company facilitating a transaction between a buyer and a seller of securities. Brokers are regulated under federal and state securities laws, and registered with the National As-

sociation of Securities Dealers and the exchange on which the securities are traded. *See Chapter 4: Section 16 Filings: Brokers.*

Broker Assisted Same-Day Sale
See "Same-Day Sale."

Brokerage Arrangement
See "Same-Day Sale."

Bull Market
Strong securities market characterized by rising prices.

Burn Rate
Also called run rate, the rate at which a company issues equity compensation, commonly calculated as either (1) options granted annually, as a percentage of either the total number of options authorized or shares outstanding; (2) total equity awards granted annually divided by the number of common shares outstanding (calculation used by ISS).

ISS recommends voting against companies with high burn rates over an average three-year period, with "high" defined as where the most recent three-year burn rate exceeds both (1) two percent of the common shares outstanding and (2) one standard deviation of its Global Industry Classification Standard (GICS by Standard & Poor and Morgan Stanley Capital International) based on Russell 3000 index or non-Russell 3000 index.

The ISS burn rate policy applies to companies with at least three years of grant activity, which eliminates IPO companies and companies emerging from bankruptcy. For mergers of equals, burn rates for both companies are averages; in acquisition situations, the acquiring company's burn rate is used.

See Chapter 2: Basic Calculations: Burn Rate.

Buyback
A company's purchase on the open market of its own stock, generally to reduce dilution.

Call Option
Derivative security conferring the right to buy a stated number of securities at a fixed price. Employee stock options are a form of call option. The converse of a put option.

Cancellation
(1) Under a stock option plan, a transaction in which an outstanding option grant is declared invalid and the unissued shares subject to the grant are returned to the stock option pool.

(2) The process by which a securities certificate is physically marked to show that it no longer represents a claim against the issuer and also voided on the records of the transfer agent.

Canceled Shares
Shares or optioned shares that have been canceled and returned to the stock option pool. This term generally also covers shares that have been forfeited or have expired.

Cap Table
Capitalization table, listing the assets of the company or corporation, usually in tabular form.

Capital Asset
Tax term describing property eligible for preferential tax treatment at capital gains rates as opposed to regular income tax rates upon disposition.

Capital Gain
Profit (proceeds received less the asset's cost basis) realized upon disposition of a capital asset. Capital assets held for one year or less result in short-term capital gain; capital assets held for more than one year result in long-term capital gain.

Capital Loss
Loss (an asset's cost basis minus the proceeds received) realized upon disposition of a capital asset. Capital assets held for one year or less result in short-term capital loss; capital assets held for more than one year result in long-term capital loss.

Capital Loss Limitation
As of September 2005, up to $3,000 of ordinary income can be offset by capital losses; additional capital losses can be carried forward to future years.

Capital Stock
Equity securities in a corporation representing basic ownership interest in the corporation, typically including the rights to vote, elect directors, and receive dividends. When only one class of stock is outstanding, the term can be used interchangeably with common stock.

Capitalization
All of the securities that have been issued by a corporation, both equity and debt. Represents the amount of capital that has been raised by the purchase of the securities.

Capitalization Table
See "Cap Table."

Captive Broker
The broker authorized to handle all stock option activity for a company; all stock plan transactions must go through this broker.

Career Shares
Term used to describe stock grants with a holding requirement for the duration of employment with the company.

Cash Bonus Plan
The payment of cash bonuses at a specified target date or event.

Cash Bonus Plan Linked to Stock-Based Award
The payment of a cash bonus conditioned upon the vesting of a stock-based award or triggered by the exercise of an option. A linked cash bonus facilitates the exercise of an option with no

cash outlay, similar to an SAR, but the recipient receives the entire equity portion of the award, not just the appreciation value.

Cashless Exercise
Method of exercising an employee stock option in which the exercise price for the shares being purchased is paid with shares of stock or a promissory note rather than with cash. See also "Same-Day-Sale," "Stock Swap."

CCC (CIK Confirmation Code)
EDGAR access code used in conjunction with the CIK to confirm filing authorization.

CCH
CCH Incorporated is an organization that reports, explains, and analyzes tax and business law, producing related publications and software.

Central Index Key
See "CIK."

CEO
See "Chief Executive Officer."

CEP
See "Certified Equity Professional."

CEPI
See "Certified Equity Professional Institute."

Certificate
Legal document providing physical, official evidence of ownership of a specific number of securities of a corporation. See "DWAC."

Certificate Number
Unique identification number or serial number assigned or affixed to each securities certificate by an issuer or transfer agent.

Certified Equity Professional (CEP)
Certification conferred upon successful completion of three levels of competency exams administered by the Certified Equity Professional Institute. The CEP designation is the standard of competence for stock plan professionals.

Certified Equity Professional Institute (CEPI)
A program of Santa Clara University's Leavey School of Business and Administration that administers the Certified Equity Professional testing and confers the Certified Equity Professional designation.

Certified Public Accountant
Certification conferred by the American Institute of Certified Public Accountants upon successful completion of four sections of competency exams as well as certain educational and profes-

sional experience requirements. Exams and requirements may vary from state to state. Standard of competence for accountants.

CFO
See "Chief Financial Officer."

Chairman of the Board
The leader of the board of directors of a company responsible for running corporate meetings and with oversight over all company operations. See "Chief Executive Officer," "President."

Change in Capitalization
Any adjustment to the capital structure of a company. See "Capitalization," "Stock Split," "Reverse Stock Split."

Change in Control
A corporation's switch to a new ownership structure, most often as the result of a merger, consolidation, acquisition, or stock or asset sale. Most stock option plans define "change in control" as it pertains to the plan, and outline the consequences to optionees and shareholders.

Cheap Stock
Pre-IPO stock options granted at an exercise price deemed by the SEC to be too low relative to the planned IPO price. This most often occurs when a prepublic company fails to upwardly adjust its FMV at a steep enough ramp to account for a higher initial asking price than anticipated. The SEC may, upon determination that "cheap stock" has been issued, impose penalties upon the company and shareholders resulting in fines or additional taxes owed.

Chief Executive Officer (CEO)
Corporate officer responsible for all of a company's operations. The CEO typically reports to the board of directors, and in smaller companies, can also be the same person as the president or the chair of the board of directors.

Chief Financial Officer (CFO)
Corporate officer responsible for a company's financial planning and recordkeeping. The CFO typically reports to the chief executive officer and is often a member of the board of directors.

Chief Information Officer (CIO)
Executive responsible for management of a company's information technology. The CIO typically reports to either the chief executive officer or chief financial officer.

Chief Operating Officer (COO)
Corporate officer responsible for management of a company's daily activities. The COO typically reports to the chief executive officer and, in smaller companies, can also be the same person as the president.

Chief Technical Officer (CTO)
Also "Chief Technology Officer," the executive responsible for a company's technical issues. This title is less uniformly applied than many other corporate titles, which can cause confusion

between industries. The CTO is sometimes also the chief information officer, and typically reports to the chief executive officer.

CIK (Central Index Key)
Public number used to uniquely identify companies and individuals filing reports with the SEC. Assigned by the SEC at the time of initial application, CIKs can be looked up on the SEC's website.

CIK Confirmation Code
See "CCC."

CIO
See "Chief Information Officer."

Class of Stock
Companies often issue more than one type, or class, of stock, such as common stock, preferred stock, convertible preferred, etc. The different classes of stock often hold different voting or dividend rights.

Clawback
Provision in some option grants that requires any stock option gains to be returned to the company if the optionee goes to work for a direct competitor within a given amount of time after either termination or the date of exercise. In many cases, appears in a clause that becomes effective if a noncompete agreement is ruled invalid.

Clearing
Post-trade and pre-settlement matching of transaction details to confirm the validity of the trade and allow settlement.

Cliff Vesting
Vesting schedule for a compensatory stock option where either (1) all of the shares subject to the stock option vest on the same date, or (2) a substantial portion of the shares subject to the option vest on the same date, with vesting continuing at regular intervals to follow (e.g., one-year cliff, followed by monthly vesting). Often used as a retention strategy or hedge against rapid turnover.

Closed Window
See "Blackout Period."

Closely Held Company
See "Private Company."

Code
See "Internal Revenue Code."

Code V
Code used in Box 12 of the W-2 to report the spread on a NSO exercise.

COLA
See "Cost of Living Adjustment."

Collateral
Property surrendered to secure a promissory note.

Commission
The fee charged for performing a transaction.

Common Stock
Equity securities representing basic ownership interest in a specific corporation. Common stock is traded on securities markets and typically provides to its holders the rights to vote, elect directors, and receive dividends. When only one class of stock is outstanding, the term can be used interchangeably with "capital stock." Differs from "preferred stock" in that no priority is received in regard to payment of dividends or asset distribution.

Compensation
Money and property given to employees, contractors, or consultants in exchange for work or governance.

Compensation Committee
Committee appointed by the board of directors of a company, generally composed solely of two or more outside directors, that sets option grant guidelines and approves specific grants for executives.

Compensation Deduction
Expense incurred by a corporation in connection with compensation that is deductible by the corporation for income tax purposes.

Compensation Element
Amount reportable in W-2 wages as compensation income as the result of a stock option exercise.

Compensation Expense
(1) For financial statement purposes, the amount recognized on a company's financial statements under either the APB 25 intrinsic value method or the FAS 123/FAS 123R fair value method with respect to securities issued in connection with stock-based compensation.

(2) For tax purposes, the amount deductible by a company in connection with an option exercise, usually in an amount equal to the amount reported by the optionee as ordinary income.

Compensation Income
Income recognized by an employee as a result of compensation paid to the employee. Any income recognized as the result of either the exercise of a nonstatutory option, or the disqualifying disposition of an incentive stock option will be considered compensation income. Compensation income is taxed as ordinary income and is typically, but not always, subject to withholding. See "Compensation Element."

Compliance
Conformity or agreement with relevant federal or regional laws and regulations, most often securities-related.

Compliance Officer
Corporate officer with primary responsibility for overseeing compliance with securities laws. This often includes establishing and documenting compliance procedures, establishing trading windows and blackout periods, and monitoring pre-clearance programs and insider trading.

Constructive Exchange Stock Swap
An option exercise in which the optionee surrenders previously owned shares to pay the option price. In a constructive exchange, the surrendered shares are not actually delivered to the company and only the new net shares over the number surrendered are actually issued. See "Stock Swap."

Contingently Issuable Shares
Shares issuable for little or no cash consideration upon the satisfaction of certain conditions; stock options. *See Chapter 2: Accounting Overview: FAS 128.*

Contingently Returnable Shares
Shares subject to recall until certain conditions have been satisfied; restricted stock. *See Chapter 2: Accounting Overview: FAS 128.*

Contractor
See "Independent Contractor."

Control Person
A director, executive officer, or other person with authority over the strategic policies, direction, and operation of a company. See "Affiliate."

Control Stock
Stock held by company affiliates that must be sold in reliance upon Rule 144.

Conversion
The process of exchanging one company's shares for another's.

Convertible Stock
Preferred stock that is convertible into the common stock of a company, at a predetermined ratio, either at the owner's discretion or at some predetermined trigger event such as an IPO.

COO
See "Chief Operating Officer."

Corporate Action
Restructuring of the company's ownership, most often through a conversion or stock split.

Corporate Governance
Broadly describes the administration, direction, and control of a corporation by its shareholders, management, board of directors, and other interested parties. Includes goals as well as relevant laws and customs.

Corporation
A legal entity with the authority to act independently from the individual shareholders who make it up, and that has the right to issue stock and exist in perpetuity.

Cost of Living Adjustment (COLA)
Annual compensation adjustment made to account for inflation.

Cox-Ross-Rubenstein Binomial Model
Mathematical formula developed by J. Cox, S. Ross, and M. Rubenstein in 1979 to value options traded on American commodity exchange: arguably one of the most well known multi-period binomial models. See "Black-Scholes Option Pricing Model"

CPA
See "Certified Public Accountant."

CTO
See "Chief Technical Officer."

CUSIP Number
Committee on Uniform Securities Identification Procedures unique identification number consisting of nine characters (letters and numbers) assigned to each securities issue, identifying both the company/issuer and the type of security being issued.

D&O
Directors and officers of a company.

D&O Liability Insurance
Insurance taken out by the company against the possibility of defending lawsuits against its directors and officers in their role as corporate managers; designed to help protect both the assets of the company and of the individual.

D&O Questionnaire
Questionnaire periodically sent to directors and officers (corporate insiders) querying them about equity holdings in company securities.

Date of Exercise
See "Exercise Date."

Date of Grant
See "Grant Date."

Death

The cessation of life. All forms of equity compensation, regardless of statutory requirements regulating transferability, become transferable upon the holder's death. The finer details of probate or other estate transactions are not discussed below, merely the broader scope of procedural, tax, and regulatory implications.

In the event of the death of an optionee or shareholder of company stock, it is important to be careful to have all appropriate documentation in hand before executing any transfer of legal title. Obviously, a death certificate should be requested, as well as any testamentary documents supporting the requested transfer. In community property states, the surviving spouse is considered to own outright half of the options granted to the optionee as of the time of grant.

ISOs are transferable to an estate or beneficiaries on death, and are subject only to plan-indicated time limits on post-death exercise. If ISO stock was acquired pursuant to an ISO or ESPP before death, the transfer is not an ISO disqualifying disposition.

If ISO stock was acquired before death, the holding period requirement for capital gains tax treatment is waived. The cost basis of ISO stock is also stepped-up at death to include the option spread at the time of death. For ISOs unexercised at death but exercised by the estate, the resultant shares must be held for at least one year to qualify for long-term capital gains tax treatment. The cost basis of unexercised ISOs is stepped-up so that at exercise, the estate's basis in the shares is equal to the sum of the exercise price plus the FMV of the option at the time of death.

NSOs unexercised at death but exercised by the estate constitute an item of "income in respect of the decedent," where the estate is not entitled to a stepped-up basis in the value of the option, and the resultant shares must be held for at least one year to qualify for long-term capital gains tax treatment. The estate recognizes ordinary income in the amount of the spread at exercise, then receives an income tax deduction for the amount of estate taxes paid on the spread at death, so when the stock is sold, the estate recognizes capital gain based on the difference between the sale price and the sum of the exercise price and the amount of ordinary income recognized.

ISOs held by dead people result in no tax consequence to the employer corporation, but their exercise does necessitate reporting on Form 6039 in January of the year following the year of exercise. The employer corporation is entitled to a tax deduction in the amount of the spread at NSO exercise, and any income realized by the estate due to the exercise must be reported on a 1099-MISC. Withholding for FICA purposes is required if the NSO is exercised in the same calendar year as the optionee's death, with any FICA wages as the result of the exercise reported on the optionee's final W-2.

Section 16 insiders cease to be insiders upon death, so a transfer of an option to the estate is not subject to short-swing profit recovery for 12 months after death. Thereafter, the estate can be subject if it is a 10% owner. If an heir is already an insider, any acquisition of shares as a beneficiary is not a 16(b) purchase. If the beneficiary becomes an insider as a result of the death, he or she must comply with 16(b) after the transfer. If an insider acts as the representative of an estate, any transactions by the insider for the benefit of the estate are exempt from 16(b) for 12 months; thereafter transactions continue to be exempt unless the estate itself is a 10% owner.

Debt Security
Certificate of indebtedness. Security issued by a borrower, includes debentures, promissory notes, bonds, or certificates of deposit. Debt securities carry interest and have a limited and specific term to maturity, at which time the security holders must be repaid.

Deduction
For tax purposes, any expense subtracted from adjusted gross income when calculating taxable income.

Deemed Execution Date
For Section 16 purposes, the date on which an insider is notified of an intra-plan transfer or certain transactions under Rule 10b5-1 plans, on which the Form 4 filing time period begins. The deemed execution date must not be more than three business days following the actual transaction date.

Deemed Transaction Date
See "Deemed Execution Date."

Deferred Tax Asset (DTA)
Accounting term describing the expected tax deduction recorded on the company's books at the time any form of equity compensation is granted for which a tax deduction may be expected under normal circumstances. Equity awards such as ISOs, where a tax deduction may be anticipated based on past disqualifying disposition history, do not generate DTAs as the tax deduction is merely anticipated, not expected. DTAs are calculated at the time of grant as (compensation expense) x (corporate tax rate) and recorded over the same service period as the corresponding compensation expense. See "Additional Paid-In Capital."

Delisting
The process whereby a company withdraws its securities from trading on an exchange either by choice or due to not meeting requirements for remaining on the exchange. Delisted stocks are generally still available for over-the-counter trading on the Pink Sheets.

Deposit/Withdrawal at Custodian
See "DWAC."

Depository Trust Company (DTC)
Central repository for securities where stocks and bonds are exchanged electronically, eliminating the need for physical movement of certificates. See "DWAC."

Deregistering
The process whereby a company files with the SEC to remove itself from registration under Section 12 of the 1934 Act, thereby ceasing to be responsible for filing and reporting requirements and ceasing to have its securities publicly traded. This process is also known as "going private" as opposed to registering to "go public."

Derivative Security
Any right—such as an option, warrant, or stock appreciation right—that derives its value from the value of an equity security.

Diluted Earnings per Share
Diluted earnings per share adjusts basic earnings per share (EPS) by increasing the denominator to include additional shares outstanding if dilutive potential common shares (debt/equity instruments convertible into common shares, warrants, options, unvested stock, rights granted under employee share plans, and contingently issuable shares) have been issued. *See Chapter 2: Accounting Overview: FAS 128.*

Dilution
The reduction in shareholder ownership interest caused by increasing the number of stock shares outstanding, whether through the granting of stock options or issuance of stock.

Direct Ownership
For Section 16 purposes, securities owned directly by an executive officer, director, or principal shareholder of a publicly owned company.

Director
Member of a board of directors.

Discounted Options
Stock options granted with an exercise price below fair market value at the time of grant.

Disposition
Sale, gift, exchange, or transfer of legal title of securities.

Disqualifying Disposition
Disposition of qualified shares (ISO/ESPP) made within two years of the date of grant/ enrollment or one year from date of exercise/purchase, causing the shares to lose their qualified status. Upon a disqualifying disposition, the employee recognizes taxable ordinary income and the company is entitled to a corresponding tax deduction in the same amount. See "Qualifying Disposition."

Dividend
Payment representing a distribution of earnings made in cash or stock by a company to its shareholders of record.

Divorce
The legal dissolution of a marriage. The treatment of equity compensation in the event of a divorce is never cut and dry, but vested equity instruments are for the most part distributed according to court order without incident. Equitable distribution of stock options and other unvested or nontransferable instruments is, however, more difficult to administer and should be confirmed with your legal counsel before executing.

Transfers of stock options are dependent upon the nature of the stock option and the state of residence. It has happened that courts may order the division of nontransferable stock options. If you are presented with such a situation, bring it directly to your legal counsel. If the company allows the transfer, you may proceed. If the company refuses to allow the transfer, the court cannot order the transfer of a stock option and you must give the handling of this process to your legal counsel.

In a community-property state, division of an option between an employee and a former spouse is not a transfer but just a re-registration of legal title. This re-registration must occur within one year after the judicial termination of the marriage or be "related" to the termination of the marriage. Regardless, be sure to have all appropriate documentation in hand before executing any transfer of legal title. Your stock tracking program should allow you to create a "phantom" employment record for the nonemployee former spouse (NFS) to facilitate reporting and withholding requirements.

In a separate-property state, it is possible that an option cannot be split unless it is a TSO. In this case, the company cannot permit a transfer of an option to the nonemployee former spouse even pursuant to a divorce decree, therefore ex-spouses must agree that the employee will exercise on behalf of the nonemployee former spouse, with a subsequent transfer of stock.

On exercise of ISOs by the NFS, no withholding is required. When the NFS exercises NSOs, withholding for applicable federal, state, and local taxes must be paid but can be used as a credit when computing income taxes and the spread is reportable as compensation income on a 1099-MISC. Withholding for Social Security and Medicare is also required on exercise of NSOs, in the same way as if the options had been exercised by the employee "as and when the wages are taken into account for FICA tax purposes" (since wages over a defined amount are not subject to the Social Security part of FICA).

For the employer corporation, withholding for applicable federal, state, and local taxes, Social Security, Medicare, and FUTA is required upon exercise of a NSO by the NFS.

Transfers of stock between spouses and ex-spouses are nonevents under the Internal Revenue Code, regardless of their status as NSO or ISO. If ISO, however, the portion received by the nonemployee former spouse retains the same preferential tax treatment as the portion retained by the employee so long as the disposition occurs not more than one year after the divorce or by divorce decree no more than six years after the divorce.

Acquisition and/or disposition of securities pursuant to a domestic relations order are exempt from reporting under Section 16(b), so there are no reporting consequences for Section 16 insiders

DJIA
See "Dow Jones Industrial Average"

Dow Jones Industrial Average (DJIA)
Market index made up of the current price-weighted averaged value of the stock of 30 companies traded on the NYSE. The DJIA was established by Charles Dow in 1884 to help investors determine the overall direction of the market at any given time. Maintained and reviewed by editors of the Wall Street Journal, the DJIA is meant to serve as a measure of the entire US market and so is composed of companies from widely diverse industries.

DTA
See "Deferred Tax Asset."

DTC
See "Depository Trust Company."

Dual Basis Asset
An asset with one basis for regular income tax purposes and another for AMT purposes.

Due Diligence
Term for the pre-IPO investigation by underwriters and their counsel into the legal, financial, and business affairs of a company. Also applies more generally to legal and financial research into other financial transactions, such as mergers and acquisitions.

DWAC (Deposit/Withdrawal at Custodian)
Process by which stock is electronically issued into a brokerage account or transferred between accounts with no physical certification. See "Certificate."

Early Exercise
The exercise of stock options in advance of vesting. The underlying stock received at exercise is subject to repurchase by the company until vesting is complete. For income tax and regulatory purposes, holding periods begin at the time of exercise.

Earnings per Share (EPS)
Basic EPS is computed by dividing reported earnings available to common stockholders by weighted average shares outstanding. Diluted EPS adjusts basic EPS by increasing the denominator to include additional shares outstanding if dilutive potential common shares had been issued, as determined under the treasury stock method. See "FAS 128." *See also Chapter 2: Accounting Overview: FAS 128.*

EDGAR
Securities and Exchange Commission's "Electronic Data Gathering, Analysis, and Retrieval" system, through which companies electronically file reports and registration statements. EDGAR is used for filing most forms or reports required under the 1933 Act or 1934 Act; to search for basic company and insider information, and real-time company and individual filings; and more. EDGAR and information about it are available on the SEC's Web site at *www.sec.gov/edgar.shtml. See Chapter 4: EDGAR.*

EDGAR Access Codes
Every company and insider has a unique set of EDGAR access codes. The CIK (Central Index Key) is a public number used to uniquely identify companies and individuals filing reports with the SEC; the CCC (CIK Confirmation Code) is used in conjunction with the CIK to confirm filing authorization; a Password is used to log onto the EDGAR system, submit filings, and change CCC; the PMAC (Password Modification Authorization Code) allows one to change one's password; and a Passphrase is used to create or change a CCC, Password, or PMAC. *See Chapter 4: EDGAR.*

EFT
See "Electronic Funds Transfer."

EITF
Emerging Issues Task Force. Task force established by the FASB to resolve interpretative matters.

EITF Issue No. 00-23
FASB Emerging Issues Task Force publication "Issues Related to the Accounting for Stock Compensation Under APB Opinion No. 25 and FASB Interpretation No. 44," issued 2000. Provides further guidance and clarification of issues raised by APB 25 and FIN 44. *See Chapter 2: Accounting Overview: EITF Issue No. 00-23.*

Electronic Funds Transfer
The movement of funds electronically.

Employee
Any person providing services for an entity, subject to the entity's legal right to control over both the work being done and the manner in which the work is to be done. For tax purposes, anyone providing a service to the company whose income must be reported on Form W-2. For accounting purposes, the term "employee" also includes outside directors.

Employee Income Retirement Security Act (ERISA)
1974 law regulating retirement plan investment and administration.

Employee Stock Option
See "Stock Option," "Incentive Stock Option," "Statutory Stock Option," "Nonstatutory Stock Option."

Employee Stock Purchase Plan (ESPP)
Broad-based stock option plan allowing employees to purchase company stock, usually through payroll deductions, according to a subscription agreement, most often at a discount. Plans that meet specific requirements are tax-qualified under Section 423 of the Internal Revenue Code. *See Chapter 3: Employee Stock Purchase Plan Basics; Chapter 3: Nonqualified Employee Stock Purchase Plans; Chapter 3: Qualified Employee Stock Purchase Plans.*

Employer
Entity retaining the services of an employee.

Employer Loans
Loans granted to employees by their employer, often in connection with the purchase of company securities. Employer loans to executives are prohibited under Section 402(a) of the Sarbanes-Oxley Act of 2002. See "Nonrecourse Note," "Recourse Note." *See also Chapter 3: Award Purchase Financing.*

End-of-Period Holdings
Refers to the contents of Form 4/Form 5 Table I.5, "Amount of Securities Beneficially Owned Following Reported Transaction(s)," or Form 4/Form 5, Table II.9, "Number of Derivative Securities Beneficially Owned Following Reported Transaction(s)." See "Form 4," "Form 5."

Enrollment
Signing up to allow payroll deductions and participate in an ESPP.

Enrollment Date
First day of the ESPP offering period, same as "grant date" for the ESPP option.

EPS
See "Earnings per Share."

Equity Compensation
Remuneration for services distributed in the form of ownership interest in the company.

Equity Security
Type of security conferring ownership interest in a company.

ERISA
See "Employee Retirement Income Security Act."

Escheatment
The process by which unclaimed or abandoned property is turned over to a state authority. Any stock or equity property is presumed abandoned after the three- to five-year period of inactivity after a dividend, stock split, or other distribution is unclaimed, or the second mailing of a statement of account or other notification or communication is returned as undeliverable.

During the abandonment period, the financial institution involved is required to try to return the property to its rightful owner. Transfer agents are required to conduct an initial search between three and twelve months after the security holder is classified as lost, then a second search between six and twelve months after the initial search, unless the total value of the property is less than $25, the transfer agent has received documentation of the death of the security holder, or the security holder is not a natural person.

If the searches are unsuccessful, the property is turned over to the state's abandoned property division or unclaimed property office, and held indefinitely for the rightful owner to claim.

Escheatment Rule
See "Securities Exchange Act of 1934, Rule 17Ad-17."

ESPP
See "Employee Stock Purchase Plan," "Internal Revenue Code, Section 423."

ESPP Option
Employee's right to participate in an ESPP offering period.

ESPP Stock
Stock acquired through participation in an ESPP.

Evergreen Provision
Evergreen provisions provide automatic increases in the number of shares available under the issuer's plan, either as a specific number or shares or for a percentage of outstanding shares; they may continue for the life of the plan or for a stated limited number of years. These eliminate the need for the company to ask shareholders for additional shares on a regular basis; supplemental share increases can be requested as needed.

As the maximum aggregate number of shares available under an ISO or ESPP plan must be known, a sample evergreen provision might read, "on January 11 of each year, the lesser of 200,000 shares or 1% of all shares outstanding on January 10 of each year will be added to the plan," so that the maximum number of shares may be calculated.

Exchange
See "Securities Exchange."

Exchange Act
See "Securities Exchange Act of 1934."

Exercisable
Adjective describing stock options for which the option holder is currently eligible to purchase the underlying stock. Options most often become exercisable as they vest, but early exercise may be permitted.

Exercise
The purchase of the stock underlying a stock option; the execution of the terms of an equity award resulting in the issuance of stock to the award holder.

Exercise Date
Date on which the stock underlying an equity award is purchased, i.e., the option is exercised.

Exercise Notice
Document submitted to a company setting forth the optionee's intent to exercise any portion of a stock option.

Exercise Period
Period within the ESPP offering period, that ends on an exercise date on which stock is purchased for all participants.

Exercise Price
The price per share at which a stock option is granted and that must be paid to purchase the stock underlying a stock option, typically fair market value of the underlying stock on the date of grant. Private companies are required to make a good faith effort to determine the fair market value when setting the exercise price of ISOs. Also called "grant price," "strike price," or "option price."

Expensing Options
Accounting term for showing the value of stock options as an expense on the company's income statement. Also referred to as showing a charge to earnings.

Expiration Date
The last date on which a stock option or other derivative security can be exercised.

Expired Grants
Stock option grants or other awards that are outstanding but no longer exercisable because the expiration date has passed.

Face Value
Number of shares multiplied by the share price.

Fair Market Value (FMV)
The value of an equity security as determined by supply and demand. For public companies, the FMV is based on the current price at which the stock is trading and is known as the stock price. For private companies, the FMV is determined as needed or on a set schedule, generally by the board of directors or a subset thereof. See "Fair Value."

Fair Value
The inherent value of an equity award, also reported as fair market value as determined by supply and demand. Defined as the intrinsic value of the award plus the time value relative to money plus the time value relative to volatility. The method of estimating the fair value of an equity award varies by the type of award; stock options and their equivalents are valued using option pricing models such as Black-Scholes. See "Binomial Option Pricing Model," "Black-Scholes Option Pricing Model."

Fair Value Accounting
Accounting method under FAS 123 in which stock options are valued using an option pricing model to determine the fair value of each equity award. See "Binomial Option Pricing Model," "Black-Scholes Option Pricing Model," "Intrinsic Value Accounting." *See also Chapter 2: Accounting Overview: FAS 123.*

Family Medical Leave Act of 1993
Allows extended leaves of absence from work to handle family issues or illness with the right to reemployment guaranteed by statute.

FAS
Financial Accounting Standard, issued by the Financial Accounting Standards Board.

FAS 109
Financial Accounting Standard No. 109, "Accounting for Income Taxes," issued by the Financial Accounting Standards Board in 1992 to establish financial accounting and reporting standards for the effects of a company's current and previous year income taxes, requiring an asset and liability approach.

FAS 123
Financial Accounting Standard No. 123, "Accounting for Stock-Based Compensation," issued in 1995, effective for fiscal years ending on or after December 15, 1996; replaced by FAS 123R in December 2004. Outlines a reporting structure initially meant to replace APB 25, but currently provided as an optional alternative. Requires companies to place a "fair value" on stock-based

compensation, either reflected as a compensation expense over the service period, or disclosed in a financial statement footnote discussing the pro forma impact that accounting under FAS 123 would have on net income and earnings per share for companies reporting under APB 25.

See Chapter 2: Accounting Overview: FAS 123.

FAS 123R
Financial Accounting Standard No. 123R, "Share-Based Payment," is a revision of FAS 123, "Accounting for Stock-Based Compensation," issued in December 2004; supersedes and eliminates the alternate use of intrinsic-value-based accounting under APB Opinion 25. FAS 123, as originally issued, is effective until FAS 123R becomes effective.

FAS 123R becomes effective as follows: (1) for public entities that do not file as small business issuers, as of the beginning of the first interim or annual reporting period that begins after June 15, 2005; (2) for public entities that file as small business issuers, as of the beginning of the first interim or annual reporting period that begins after December 15, 2005; (3) for nonpublic entities, as of the beginning of the first annual reporting period that begins after December 15, 2005.

See Chapter 2: Accounting Overview: FAS 123R

FAS 128
Financial Accounting Standard No. 128, "Earnings per Share," issued by the Financial Accounting Standards Board in 1997 to establish standards for calculating and presenting Earnings Per Share. Requires that entities present on the face of their income statements: (1) basic EPS for income from continuing operations and for net income; (2) diluted EPS for income from continuing operations and for net income (unless there are no dilutive instruments issued, meaning only common stock is outstanding).

See Chapter 2: Accounting Overview: FAS 128

FAS 148
Financial Accounting Standard No. 148, "Accounting for Stock-Based Compensation—Transition and Disclosure, an Amendment of FASB Statement No. 123," issued in December 2002. Outlines three alternative methods for companies to make the transition from accounting for stock options under APB 25 to accounting for stock options under FAS 123. Expands disclosure requirements.

FAS 150
Financial Accounting Standard No. 150, "Accounting for Certain Financial Instruments with Characteristics of both Liabilities and Equity," issued in May 2003. Sets standards for classifying and measuring any equity instrument that is mandatorily redeemable or that requires a company to repurchase its stock as a liability. FASB Staff Position (FSP) 150-3 indefinitely deferred the effective date for mandatorily redeemable instruments issued by nonpublic entities not registered with the SEC and for certain mandatorily redeemable controlling interests.

FASB
See "Financial Accounting Standards Board."

Fed
See "Federal Reserve Board."

Federal Income Tax (FIT)
Taxes paid to the federal government on the basis of earned (compensatory) income.

Federal Insurance Contributions Act (FICA)
Tax on employers and employees, used to fund the Social Security system and Medicare.

Federal Reserve Board
Board of Governors of the Federal Reserve System. Governors are nominated by the president of the United States and confirmed by the U.S. Senate to 14-year terms. No two governors may come from the same Federal Reserve district.

Federal Reserve District
Any one of the 12 areas served by Federal Reserve banks. The banks are located in Boston; New York; Philadelphia; Cleveland; Richmond, Va.; Atlanta; Chicago; St. Louis; Minneapolis; Kansas City, Mo.; Dallas; and San Francisco. See "Federal Reserve System."

Federal Reserve Regulation T
See "Regulation T."

Federal Reserve System
The central bank of the United States, created by the Federal Reserve Act in 1913. Consists of a central governmental agency, the Board of Governors, in Washington, D.C., and 12 Federal Reserve banks located in Boston; New York; Philadelphia; Cleveland; Richmond, Va.; Atlanta; Chicago; St. Louis; Minneapolis; Kansas City, Mo.; Dallas; and San Francisco.

Federal Unemployment Tax Act (FUTA)
Tax imposed on employers to provide benefits for workers during brief periods of unemployment.

FICA
See "Federal Insurance Contributions Act."

FIFO
First-in-first-out. Describes a process used to calculate gain or loss results of a securities sale. In an account holding shares of stock purchased at different times at different prices, any sale of securities is assumed to be the sale of stock from first purchased to most recently purchased unless the seller otherwise specifies which shares were sold.

FIN 28
FASB Interpretation No. 28, "Accounting for Stock Appreciation Rights and Other Variable Stock Option or Award Plans," issued December 1978. Provides interpretation of APB Opinions 15 and 25. *See Chapter 2: Accounting Overview: FIN 28.*

FIN 44
FASB Interpretation No. 44, "Accounting for Certain Transactions Involving Stock Compensation, an Interpretation of APB Opinion No. 25," issued March 2000. Provides additional guidance and clarification to issues raised under APB 25. See Chapter 2: Accounting Overview: FIN 44.

Financial Accounting Standards Board (FASB)
Private organization that succeeded the Accounting Principles Board in 1973 in developing and establishing GAAP by issuing opinions and decisions. Officially recognized as authoritative by both the Securities and Exchange Commission (SEC) and the American Institute of Certified Public Accountants (AICPA).

Releases Statements of Financial Accounting Standards (FAS) to establish new standards or amend those previously issued; Statements of Financial Accounting Concepts, which set forth fundamentals on which future financial accounting and reporting standards will be based; Interpretations (FIN), which clarify, explain, or elaborate on existing practice; Technical Bulletins (FTB) providing guidance on implementation and practice problems; Exposure Drafts, which are proposed FAS or Interpretations issued for public comment prior to adoption; Discussion Memorandums and Invitations to Comment on major topics for public comment; Research Reports; and Special Reports.

First-In-First-Out
See "FIFO."

Fiscal Year
A 12-month accounting period that begins the day a company starts a new accounting year. Fiscal years typically begin at calendar year quarters: January 1, April 1, July 1, or October 1, but the first day of a fiscal year can fall on any predetermined date.

FIT
See "Federal Income Tax."

Fixed Award
Under APB 25, an equity award where the measurement date is the grant date and as such, the compensation expense is fixed as of the date of grant. See "Variable Award."

Fixed Plan
Under APB 25, a stock plan where both the number of shares being issued and their exercise price are known on the grant date, resulting in the compensation expense being fixed or determined at issue. See "Variable Plan."

FMLA
See "Family Medical Leave Act of 1993."

FMV
See "Fair Market Value."

Forfeiture
The loss of stock options before expiration for some cause, most often termination of service or violation of a noncompete agreement.

Form 3
Initial Statement of Beneficial Ownership of Securities. Initial form filed with the SEC, the company, and the stock exchange on which the company's stock is traded.

Used to disclose the fact that a person has become a Section 16 insider, Form 3 provides detailed information on the insider's direct and indirect stock holdings, as well as any stock options, warrants, rights, and convertible stocks or bonds. Must be filed within 10 days after the event making the person an insider or by the effective date of the initial registration statement.

See Chapter 4: Section 16 Filings.

Form 4
Statement of Changes in Beneficial Ownership of Securities. Periodic form filed with the SEC, the company, and the stock exchange on which the company's stock is traded.

Used to disclose any non-exempt change and many exempt changes in the Section 16 insider's ownership of company stock. Must be filed on or before the second business day after either the day on which a change in beneficial ownership occurs or the deemed execution date of transactions qualifying for a delay in filing.

See Chapter 4: Section 16 Filings.

Form 5
Annual Statement of Changes in Beneficial Ownership of Securities. Year-end form filed with the SEC, the company, and the stock exchange on which the company's stock is traded.

Used to report any transactions that are reportable but are not required to be reported on Form 4. Also can be used to report holdings and/or changes not previously reported on Forms 3 or 4 on a delinquent basis. If required, must be filed within 45 days after the end of the issuer's fiscal year.

See Chapter 4: Section 16 Filings.

Form 8-A
Optional short form for registration of securities under Section 12 of the 1934 Act.

Form 8-K
"Current report" used to report under Section 12 of the 1934 Act the occurrence of any material events or corporate changes that are of importance to investors or security holders and previously have not been reported by the registrant. Provides more current information on certain specified events than would Forms 10-Q or 10-K.

Form 10
General form for registration of securities under Section 12 of the 1934 Act. Can be used for classes of securities of issuers for which no other form is prescribed. Requires certain business and financial information about the issuer.

Form 10-C
Must be filed by any issuer whose securities are quoted on the NASDAQ interdealer quotation system. Any change in the number of shares that exceeds 5% of the class outstanding and any change in the name of the issuer are reported on this form, which must be filed within 10 days of such change.

Form 10-K
Annual report required under Section 12 of the 1934 Act, filed with the SEC, that provides a comprehensive overview of the company's business. As a result of the Sarbanes-Oxley Act of 2002, accelerated filing deadlines applying to companies that have been subject to the periodic reporting requirements for at least 12 months, have filed at least one annual report, have a public float of at least $75 million, and are not eligible to use the small business reporting forms are phasing in as follows: fiscal years ending on or after December 31, 2004, must be filed within 75 days of the end of the company's fiscal year; on or after December 31, 2005, must be filed within 60 days after year-end.

Form 10-Q
Quarterly report required under Section 12 of the 1934 Act, filed with the SEC, that provides an ongoing view of the company's financial position during the year, and includes unaudited financial statements. Must be filed for each of the first three fiscal quarters of the company's fiscal year. As a result of the Sarbanes-Oxley Act of 2002, accelerated filing deadlines applying to companies that have been subject to the periodic reporting requirements for at least 12 months, have filed at least one annual report, have a public float of at least $75 million, and are not eligible to use the small business reporting forms are phasing in as follows: for fiscal years ending on or after December 31, 2004, must be filed within 40 days after quarter-end; on or after December 31, 2005, must be filed within 35 days after quarter-end.

Form 10-SB
General form for registration of securities under Section 12 of the 1934 Act for "small business owners" (generally U.S. or Canadian companies with revenues and public market float less than $25 million). Requires slightly less detailed information about the company's business than Form 10.

Form 11-K
Special annual report for employee stock purchase, savings, and similar plans, interests in which constitute securities registered under the 1933 Act. The Form 11-K annual report is required in addition to any other annual report of the issuer of the securities (e.g., a company's annual report to all shareholders or Form 10-K).

Form 12b-25
Notification of late filing by a reporting company that determines that it is unable to file a required periodic report when first due without unreasonable effort or expense. If a company files a Form 12b-25, it is entitled to relief, but must file the required report within five calendar days

(for a Form 10-Q or 10-QSB) or within 15 calendar days (for a Form 10-K, 10-KSB, 20-F, 11-K, or N-SAR).

Form 15
Form filed with the SEC to deregister. Available for use by companies with fewer than 300 shareholders or less than 500 persons, where the total assets of the issuer have not exceeded $10 million on the last day of each of the issuer's three most recent fiscal years, and usually done in conjunction with delisting from the exchange on which the company's securities were traded.

Form 83(b)
See "Section 83(b) Election."

Form 144
Notice of proposed sale of restricted securities or securities held by an affiliate of the issuer in reliance on Rule 144. Must be filed when the amount to be sold during any three-month period is greater than 500 shares or has an aggregate sales price greater than $10,000.

Form 1040
Internal Revenue Service standard form for filing of personal income tax.

Form 1099
Internal Revenue Service form for reporting compensation income paid to nonemployees.

Form 6251
Internal Revenue Service form on which the alternative minimum tax calculation is made. If completion of Form 6251 indicates that alternative minimum tax payment is required, the Form must be attached to Form 1040 when the individual's taxes are filed.

Form S-1
Basic form to register securities with the SEC for sale to the public. Can be used to register securities for which no other form is authorized or prescribed, except securities of foreign governments or political subdivisions thereof. See "Securities Act of 1933, Registration Statements."

Form S-2
Simplified optional registration form that permits incorporation by reference from the company's annual report to stockholders (or annual report on Form 10-K) and periodic reports. May be used by companies that have been required to report under the 1934 Act for a minimum of three years and have timely filed all required reports during the 12 months and any portion of the month immediately preceding the filing of the registration statement. See "Securities Act of 1933, Registration Statements."

Form S-3
Most simplified registration form, maximizes incorporating by reference information from 1934 Act filings. May be used only by companies that have been required to report under the 1934 Act for a minimum of 12 months and have timely filed all required reports during the 12 months and any portion of the month immediately preceding the filing of the registration statement, where the offering and issuer meet the eligibility tests prescribed by the form. See "Securities Act of 1933, Registration Statements."

Form S-4
Form for the registration of securities to be offered to a company's employees in connection with business combinations and other offers. See "Securities Act of 1933, Registration Statements."

Form S-8
Form for the registration of securities to be offered to a company's employees in connection with certain benefit plans. See "Securities Act of 1933, Registration Statements."

Form S-11
Form for the registration of securities of certain real estate companies, including real estate investment trusts. See "Securities Act of 1933, Registration Statements."

Form SB-1
Available to certain "small business issuers" (generally U.S. or Canadian companies with revenues and public market float less than $25 million) for registration of offerings of up to $10 million of securities, provided that the company has not registered more than $10 million in securities offerings during the preceding 12 months. Requires less detailed information about the issuer's business than Form S-1. See "Securities Act of 1933, Registration Statements."

Form SB-2
Available to certain "small business issuers" (generally U.S. or Canadian companies with revenues and public market float less than $25 million) for registration of securities to be sold for cash. Requires less detailed information about the issuer's business than Form S-1. See "Securities Act of 1933, Registration Statements."

Form SR
Form used by companies registering for the first time under the 1933 Act to report sales of registered securities and the use of resultant proceeds. This form is required to be filed at specified periods of time throughout the offering period and a final report is required after the termination of the offering. See "Securities Act of 1933, Registration Statements."

Form W-2
Internal Revenue Service "Wage and Tax Statement." Required to report wages earned to employees. See "Code V."

Form W-7
Internal Revenue Service "Application for IRS Individual Taxpayer Identification Number (TIN)". Used to request a TIN for any person who is not eligible for a Social Security number but who must furnish a TIN to receive wages in the United States.

Form W-8BEN
Internal Revenue Service "Certificate of Foreign Status." Required to inform any payer, broker, transfer agent, or other middleman that an employee is a nonresident alien or foreign entity not subject to either U.S. tax reporting or backup withholding rules.

Form W-9
Internal Revenue Service "Request for Taxpayer Identification Number and Certification Form." Required to furnish any payer, broker, transfer agent, or other middleman with an employee's Social Security number or taxpayer identification number.

Formula-Based Options
Any agreement between the company and the recipient in which the company agrees to grant options to the recipient on a formulaic basis. This may include options granted at a specific future date with an exercise price equal to today's FMV, but the number of options granted depends on the meeting of performance criteria, or options granted with an exercise price equal to the FMV when performance criteria have been met.

Formula Plan
Stock option plan under which the number of shares to be granted, the grant recipients, and all other terms and conditions applicable to grants are determined based on a formula specified under the plan and cannot be modified on a discretionary basis.

Free-Standing SAR
Stock appreciation right issued independently of stock options. See "SAR." *See also Chapter 3: Stock Appreciation Rights.*

Friends-and-Family Shares
Company shares reserved for purchase at the IPO price by "friends and family" of the company at the time of an IPO. Can refer to shares offered to people who have provided assistance to the company, shares offered in connection with IPO services, or shares offered to actual "friends and family" of company employees and associates.

Fully Vested
See "Vested."

FUTA
See "Federal Unemployment Tax Act."

GAAP
See "Generally Accepted Accounting Principles."

Gain
The amount realized as ordinary income on exercise of a NSO. See "Spread."

Generally Accepted Accounting Principles (GAAP)
The standards and guidelines governing the practice of financial accounting and reporting, established by opinions and decisions issued by the Financial Accounting Standards Board and the Governmental Accounting Standards Board.

Going Public
See "Initial Public Offering."

Golden Parachute
Term for the extra compensation received by executives and key employees upon a change in control of a company, often used to describe an extremely favorable severance package.

Government Printing Office (GPO)
The Government Printing Office produces and distributes federal government information products, and also maintains GPO Access at *www.gpoaccess.gov,* providing free electronic access to important federal government information products, such as the United States Code.

GPO
See "Government Printing Office."

GPO Access
See "Government Printing Office."

Graded Vesting
Compensatory stock option vesting that occurs at regular intervals.

Grant
Award issued by a corporation, either as a stock option or as stock. See "Stock Option," "Stock."

Grant Date
Date of award issuance.

Grant Number
Number assigned for record-keeping purposes to stock option grants or stock award grants.

Grant Price
See "Exercise Price."

Grant Type
Type of award in question: ISO, NSO, SAR, restricted stock, etc.

Holding Period
The period for which stock is held after a grant, exercise, or purchase. The length of the holding period can have a significant impact on the tax or securities law treatment of the stock in question. (1) For tax-qualified (ISO, ESPP) options, the holding period is two years after the date of grant and one year after the date of exercise/purchase; (2) for capital gains purposes, the holding period is one year from the date of property transfer; (3) for Rule 144 affiliates, the holding period is one year from the date the securities are paid for with Rule 144 compliance; (4) for Rule 144 nonaffiliates, the holding period is one year from the date the securities are paid for with Rule 144 compliance, two years for no compliance necessary.

Hundred Thousand Dollar Rule
See "$100,000 Rule."

Hypo Tax
"Hypothetical" tax whereby a corporation can withhold the standard taxes payable in the home country to "tax equalize" the salary of an expatriate employee.

IASB
See "International Accounting Standards Board," "IFRS 2."

ID System
See "Institutional Delivery System."

IFRS 2
International Financial Reporting Standard 2 "Share-Based Payment," released by the International Accounting Standards Board in 2004. In substantial convergence with FAS 123(R). *See Chapter 2: Accounting Overview: IFRS 2.*

Immaculate Exercise
Stock option exercise in which the amount necessary to exercise the option is calculated in terms of share value (total exercise price / FMV per share = number of shares to be surrendered). The optionee receives only the number of shares in excess of the shares surrendered as payment. No exchange of money or previously owned shares is recognized. *See Chapter 3: Award Purchase Financing: Immaculate Exercise.*

Immature ISO Stock
When an incentive stock option is exercised, the stock received is considered immature until the required ISO holding periods of one year from date of exercise and two years from date of grant have been met. Any disposition of immature ISO stock is a disqualifying disposition.

Incentive Stock Option (ISO)
A tax-qualified option meeting certain requirements outlined in Section 422 of the Internal Revenue Code, which entitles holder to favorable tax treatment upon exercise and disposition. Also regulated by Sections 421 and 424 of the Code.

See "Internal Revenue Code, Section 421," "Internal Revenue Code, Section 422," "Internal Revenue Code, Section 424." *See also Chapter 3: Incentive Stock Options.*

Independent Contractor
Any person or business providing services for an entity where the entity has no legal right to control the manner in which the work is to be done, only to specify the work to be done.

Independent Director
See "Outside Director."

Indexed Stock Options
Stock options granted with an exercise price based on either the company's stock price performance relative to a specified index or the performance of the specified index. The price typically increases over the life of the option at a fixed rate or according to some formula and remains variable until the option is exercised. Optionees profit from options only if the share price outperforms the hurdle rate built into the exercise price.

Indirect Ownership
Ownership by immediate family members of or held in trust for the benefit of an executive officer, director, or principal shareholder of a publicly owned company. Also includes shares held under employee benefit plans. See "Beneficial Ownership."

Information Statement (Regulation 14C/Schedule 14C)
Schedule 14C sets forth the disclosure requirements for information statements. Generally, a company with securities registered under Section 12 of the 1934 Act must send an information statement to every holder of the registered security who is entitled to vote on any matter for which the company is not soliciting proxies (if the company solicits proxies, Regulation 14C/Schedule 14A may be required).

Initial Public Offering (IPO)
The process whereby a private company offers its shares to the investing public and becomes a public company. Before the IPO, the company must file a registration statement with the SEC under the 1933 Act. After the IPO, the company is a public company registered under Section 12 of the 1934 Act and thus obligated to the reporting requirements therein. See "Securities Act of 1933, Registration Statements."

Insider
Any person with access to nonpublic material information about a company; most often used to refer to persons subject to Section 16 of the 1934 Act and members of their immediate families. See "Securities Exchange Act of 1934, Section 16," "Section 16 Insider."

Insider Trading
The illegal buying or selling of company stock while in possession of nonpublic material information about that company.

Insider Trading & Securities Fraud Enforcement Act of 1988 (ITSFEA)
Federal legislation that substantially increased penalties for insider trading.

Institutional Delivery System
Computerized system used by the Depository Trust Company and its major participants to send and receive automated confirmation feeds, affirmations, and reports.

Institutional Investor
Organization that invests in stock markets, most notably pension funds, insurance companies, and mutual funds.

Institutional Shareholder Services
See "ISS."

Interest
Amount borrowers pay to lenders for the privilege of using their money; usually calculated as a percentage of the amount borrowed.

Interest Rate
The percentage rate used to calculate interest payments.

In-the-Money Options
Stock options with an exercise price lower than the fair market value at any given time.

Internal Revenue Code (IRC) (Code)
The Internal Revenue Code is Title 26 of the United States Code, the federal statute providing for taxation of individuals, corporations, and other entities, and is administered and enforced by the Internal Revenue Service.

Internal Revenue Code, Section 83
Internal Revenue Code section that governs the taxation of property received in exchange for services, including income tax consequences of nonstatutory option ownership.

Internal Revenue Code, Section 83(b)
Allows election to recognize income generated by the purchase of unvested equity instruments in the year of exercise rather than at each vesting date. See "Section 83(b) Election."

Internal Revenue Code, Section 162(m)
Internal Revenue Code section that restricts the amount of income on which a company can take a tax deduction for compensation of a senior executive (CEO and the top four highly compensated employees) to $1 million. Stock options are factored into this calculation unless they are considered "performance-based compensation."

Internal Revenue Code, Section 409A
Created by the American Jobs Creation Act of 2004 to regulate nonqualified deferred compensation plans, including stock options, stock appreciation rights, and other equity compensation, IRC Section 409A is effective in regard to awards granted or vested after December 31, 2004. Notice 2005-1 was published on January 10, 2005, to provide clarification of and guidance on Section 409A.

A "nonqualified deferred compensation plan" subject to the provisions of Section 409A is defined as any plan or arrangement between the employer corporation and employees, directors, and independent contractors providing for the deferral of compensation in a plan that is not tax-qualified. These include: stock options with an exercise price less than FMV on grant date; restricted stock units and deferred stock units; performance share units with multi-year performance conditions; stock appreciation rights in all closely held companies or in any company when payable in cash; phantom stock; non-423 plan ESPPs; supplemental retirement plans; nonqualified pension plans; and severance plans permitting elections between lump sum and installment payments.

Compensation plans that are *not* subject to Section 409A include: stock options with an exercise price at least equal to FMV on grant date; restricted stock; stock-settled SARs that meet certain conditions in public companies; performance shares issued at grant and subject to forfeiture if performance conditions are not met; 423 Plan ESPPs; tax qualified retirement and tax deferred annuity plans; eligible deferred compensation plans under IRC Section 457(b); and vacation leave, sick leave, compensatory time, disability pay, and death benefit plans.

Deferrals under nonqualified deferred compensation plans may be exempt from the provisions of Section 409A if they meet the following requirements; (1) the initial deferral election (including the form of payment) is made in the calendar year before the service period, or within 30 days after initial participation in the plan unless the compensation is performance-based (performance period is at least one year and amount of bonus is contingent on meeting written performance criteria established within 90 days after the start of the period), in which case the initial deferral election can be made up to six months before the end of the performance period; (2) any subsequent change is made at least 12 months prior to the original payment date and is not effective for at least 12 months, with payment not made for at least five years from the original payment date exception in the case of death, disability, or unforeseeable emergency; (3) the plan allows distribution only on separation of service (with a six-month waiting period for key employees), disability, death, unforeseeable emergency, at a specified date or according to a schedule fixed as of the date of deferral, or on change in control as specified by IRS guidance; and (4) the plan may not permit acceleration of payment except as provided in regulations.

If the requirements for exemption are not met, the deferred compensation is taxable at the current basis as it vests, as well as being subject to increased tax equal to 20% of the original deferral plus earnings, interest at the underpayment rate (5% at October 1, 2004), plus 1% on the amount of tax that should have been paid on the amount of the original deferral plus earnings.

Deferrals under nonqualified deferred compensation plans that do not meet the requirements but are subject to a substantial risk of forfeiture (more narrowly defined than under Section 83) will not be taxable until vesting, but then will typically be subject to tax at the current basis plus an additional tax in the amount of 20% of the original deferral plus earnings.

Employer corporations will be required to include the total amount of a participant's deferred compensation on his or her annual W-2 or 1099.

Plans and agreements operated during 2005 in compliance with Section 409A and Notice 2005-1 will have until December 31, 2005 to be amended for conformity with Section 409A. Plans or agreements terminated by December 31, 2005 will not be subject to Section 409A solely as a result of the termination so long as all deferrals under the plan or agreement are distributed and included in income in 2005.

During 2005, new payment elections made by participants in deferred compensation plans with respect to deferred amounts subject to Section 409A will not be treated as changes either requiring a five year delay in payment or an impermissible acceleration of payment so long as the plan or agreement is amended by December 31, 2005 to allow the new elections. In addition, termination of participation in a deferred compensation plan or agreement subject to Section 409A will be allowed at any time during 2005 so long as the plan or agreement is amended by December 31, 2005 to allow the election to terminate and all deferrals under the plan or agreement are distributed and included in income in 2005.

Internal Revenue Code, Section 421
Sets "general rules" covering statutory (ISO or ESPP) stock options.

- A qualifying disposition of a statutory option results in no taxable income recognition at exercise and no Section 162 deduction allowance.

- A disqualifying disposition of a statutory option results in taxable income recognition to the optionee and a corresponding tax deduction recognized by the employer corporation.
- If a statutory option is exercised by an estate of a decedent, the holding period and employment requirements of Sections 422 and 423 do not apply and the estate receives a step-up in tax basis.

See "Incentive Stock Option," "Employee Stock Purchase Plan." *See also Chapter 3: Incentive Stock Options.*

Internal Revenue Code, Section 422
Sets rules for incentive stock options.

- A qualifying disposition of an ISO meets holding periods of two years from date of grant and one year from date of exercise. A disqualifying disposition fails to meet one or both criteria. A transfer due to bankruptcy under Title 11 is not considered to be a disqualifying disposition.
- The optionee must be in the continuous employ of the company or its subsidiaries from the date of grant until no more than three months before exercise or one year in the case of disability. Leaves not exceeding 90 days do not interrupt continuous employment; reemployment guaranteed leaves have no limit.
- The plan must specify the aggregate number of either all types of shares or specifically ISO shares subject to it. A maximum as a percentage of shares authorized, issued, or outstanding on the date of adoption of the plan is acceptable.
- The plan must identify the employees or class of employees eligible to receive options.
- The plan must have been approved by the company's stockholders within 12 months of adoption by the board of directors.
- The plan must not allow options to be granted more than 10 years after plan adoption/approval.
- An ISO cannot be exercised more than 10 years after the date of grant.
- The exercise price of an ISO must equal at least the FMV of the stock subject to the option at the time the option is granted.
- An ISO is not transferable and is not exercisable by anyone other than the optionee during the optionee's lifetime.
- An ISO may not be granted to a holder of more than 10% of the combined stock of the company unless it (a) cannot be exercised more than 5 years after the date of grant, and (b) must have a minimum exercise price of 110% of the FMV on the date of grant.
- $100,000 rule—Only the first $100,000 (as measured at the time of grant) of FMV of stock subject to option that first becomes exercisable in any one calendar year retains its ISO status. Options that exceed that amount automatically lose ISO treatment.

See "Incentive Stock Option." *See also Chapter 3: Incentive Stock Options.*

Internal Revenue Code, Section 423
Sets rules for tax-favored employee stock purchase plans (Section 423 ESPPs).

- A qualifying disposition of an ESPP option meets holding periods of two years from date of grant and one year from date of exercise. A disqualifying disposition fails to meet one or both criteria.
- The optionee must be in the continuous employ of the company, its parent, or subsidiaries from the date of grant until no more than three months before exercise. Leaves not exceeding 90 days do not interrupt continuous employment; re-employment guaranteed leaves have no limit. The plan must designate the corporations or class of corporations whose employees will be offered options.
- The plan must provide that options are to be granted only to the employees of the company adopting the plan or its related corporations.
- The plan must be approved by stockholders within 12 months of its adoption by the board.
- The plan must allow participation to all employees except for those specifically allowed to be excluded: (1) 5% stockholders; (2) those employed for less than two years; (3) those customarily employed for five months or less in the calendar year; (4) those customarily employed for fewer than 20 hours per week; and (5) highly compensated employees.
- The exercise price of an ESPP option must equal at least 85% of the FMV of the stock subject to the option at the time the option is either granted or exercised.
- The plan must by its terms provide that all participating employees shall have the same rights and privileges (limitations may be placed on the basis of uniform applications such as salary).
- The plan must provide for maximum duration of options: (1) if the option is priced at less than 85% of the FMV at the date of exercise, it can be exercisable for no more than five years after the date of grant; or (2) options providing alternative exercise prices can be exercisable for no more than 27 months after the date of grant.
- The plan must prohibit each participating employee from purchasing stock under all 423 plans of the employer and related corporations to the extent that the FMV of stock measured at the date of grant would exceed $25,000 for each calendar year the options remain outstanding.
- The plan must not allow for options to be transferable during the optionee's lifetime.
- At qualifying disposition of an ESPP option whose exercise price is less than the FMV at grant, the lesser of (1) the FMV at disposition less the exercise price, or (2) the FMV at grant less the exercise price, shall be recognized as compensation income.

See "Employee Stock Purchase Plan." *See also Chapter 3: Qualified Employee Stock Purchase Plans.*

Internal Revenue Code, Section 424
Provides definitions and sets special rules for stock options, statutory options, and statutory option stock. See "Incentive Stock Option," "Employee Stock Purchase Plan." *See also Chapter 3: Incentive Stock Options, Chapter 3: Qualified Employee Stock Purchase Plans.*

Internal Revenue Code, Section 6039
Requires that or before January 31 of the calendar year following either (1) an exercise of an ISO, or (2) the first transfer of legal title of stock acquired by participation in a Section 423 ESPP plan, the issuer corporation must send the stock recipient a written statement describing the transaction. Statements may be provided either physically or electronically. An extension of time not exceeding 30 days may be requested.

Internal Revenue Code, Section 6722
Provides penalties for companies not providing information statements required under Section 6039 of $50 per failure to provide either a statement or correct information, to a $100,000 annual limit. These penalties may be higher in the case of intentional disregard.

Internal Revenue Service (IRS)
Government agency charged with administration of federal tax laws (the Internal Revenue Code); a bureau of the Department of the Treasury.

Internal Revenue Service Notice
Periodic notices published to provide additional guidance or clarification to items in the internal revenue code.

Internal Revenue Service Notice 2005-1
"Transition Guidance on Section 409A" was published on January 10, 2005 to provide clarification of Section 409A of the IRC, created by the American Jobs Creation Act of 2004.

International Accounting Standards Board (IASB)
Private standards-setting organization based in London, UK; made up of members of nine countries. Works to establish GAAP as global accounting standards on an international basis and co-operates with national accounting standard-setters toward standards convergence. Issued IFRS 2 in 2004.

International Organization of Standardization
The world's largest developer of standards, ISO is a network of the national standards institutes of 148 countries. Standards produced are conformed to on a voluntary basis, but often become market requirements based on their use and demand. See "ISO 9000 Standards."

Interpretation 44
See "FIN 44."

Intrinsic Value
The advantage of holding an option rather than buying the underlying stock directly. For accounting purposes, the inherent value of an equity award, calculated as the difference between the award price and the fair market value of the underlying stock on the measurement date, generally the date of grant. See "Fair Value."

Intrinsic Value Accounting
Accounting method under APB 25 in which equity awards are valued based on the difference between the award price and the fair market value of the underlying stock on the measurement date. See "Fair Value Accounting."

IPO
See "Initial Public Offering."

IRS
See "Internal Revenue Service."

ISO
See "Incentive Stock Option," "International Organization of Standardization."

ISO Amount Limitation
See "$100,000 Rule."

ISO 9000 Standards
Established by the International Organization of Standardization, ISO 9000 refers to a family of standards addressing quality management and quality assurance systems. Voluntary compliance with ISO 9000 standards includes an independent audit of processes influencing quality to assure conformity with the relevant standard's requirements. ISO 9000 standards establish requirements that quality systems must meet, but do not dictate the manner in which they should be met.

ISS
Institutional Shareholder Services is an organization that provides proxy voting and corporate governance services to institutional investors. Also serves as a vendor, providing corporations with corporate governance tools.

Issuer
Under securities laws, a company that has sold or intends to sell its own stock.

Junior Stock Plans
Plans in which a specific class of common stock is issued to employees that is generally subordinate to common stock for voting, liquidation, and dividends. Can be convertible into common stock if performance goals are achieved or certain transactions occur.

Large Cap
Refers to either a company or the stock of a company whose market capitalization is greater than $1 billion.

Lattice Model
See "Binomial Option Pricing Model."

Leave of Absence
Any approved, temporary, absence from employment. Leaves of absence are defined in most plans, but often without adequate guidance as to how administrative details such as vesting should be handled. It is important to maintain consistency in dealing with leaves and to have a documented policy with procedures in place. A primary consideration is whether or not vesting will be allowed for the duration of the leave.

For ISO/ESPP purposes, most temporary leaves of absence (up to three months) do not disrupt the employment relationship and do not affect the statutory nature of options; a temporary layoff can qualify as a leave of absence. If the right to re-employment is guaranteed either by statute or by contract (military leave, maternity leave, FMLA, etc.), the leave can be indefinite. Where the leave exceeds three months and re-employment is not guaranteed, the employment relationship is deemed to have been terminated on the day after the third month of leave.

In the case of guaranteed re-employment indefinite leaves, be sure to obtain supporting documentation for your files. It is also important to monitor the employee's status in your stock tracking program, as many software programs will automatically terminate ISO status after the third month of leave.

Legend
The notice on a stock certificate that has been issued for restricted securities that specifies the restrictions on resale.

Legended Stock
Stock subject to restrictions on transfer, generally denoted by a descriptive legend.

Liability
As an accounting term, something that is owed to another party.

Liability Award
Under FAS 123R, any equity award whose value is based on equity, but that is paid in cash. See "Stock Appreciation Right," "Phantom Stock."

Liquidity Event
Financial transaction whereby shareholders holding stock for which there was previously no market are able to sell their shares, usually because of an IPO or acquisition.

Lockup
The period of time immediately after an IPO during which certain shares of stock cannot be sold into the public market pursuant to an agreement between the company and the underwriters. Typically lasts 180 days.

Lockup Agreement
Contract entered into by a company's shareholders agreeing to abide by the terms of the lockup as established by the public offering underwriters. Boilerplate lockup agreement language is often included in private company exercise agreements and stock purchase agreements before need to ensure compliance in the case of a public offering.

Look-Back Feature
Provision whereby the purchase price for ESPP shares is based on the lower of the FMV at the beginning of the offering period or at the end of the offering period.

Long-Term Incentive Plan (LTIP)
Any system of compensation designed to maximize employee retention and satisfaction. Generally refers to any plan granting equity awards with holding or vesting requirements.

Lost Securityholder
As defined in the Securities Exchange Act of 1934, Rule 17Ad-17, any securityholder for whom a change of address has not been filed and to whom a transfer agent sends correspondence that has been returned as undeliverable. If the correspondence has been resent within one month, the transfer agent does not have to deem the securityholder "lost" until the day the resent item is returned as undeliverable. See "Escheatment.'

Loss
The amount by which the purchase price exceeds the sale price in a securities transaction.

LTIP
See "Long-Term Incentive Plan."

M&A
Mergers and acquisitions.

Market Order
Order placed with a broker for a trade to be executed immediately at the best available price.

Margin Loans
Loans stockbrokers extend to their clients using the negotiable securities in their brokerage accounts as collateral. Regulated by Federal Reserve Regulation T. These loans generally bear interest at the margin loan rate until repaid, and may not exceed 50% of the market value of the stock in the account. If the loan comes to exceed 75% of the market value of the stock in the account due to market fluctuation or interest charges, the loan must be called and the account must be restored to the initial margin, or 50%.

Margin Requirement
The part of a security's price the buyer must pay in cash when engaging in margin trading.

Margin Trading
The purchase and sale of securities with money borrowed from brokers and dealers, collateralized by the negotiable securities in the account.

Market Cap
See "Market Capitalization"

Market Capitalization
Market value of a company, generally calculated by multiplying the share price by the number of shares outstanding. Companies are often referred to as "small-cap," "mid-cap," or "large-cap." While there are no set limits dividing the categories, small-cap stocks generally have market caps of less than $500 million, large-cap stocks generally have market caps of more than $1 billion, and mid-cap stocks are anything in between.

Mature ISO Stock
When an incentive stock option is exercised, the stock received is considered immature until the required ISO holding periods of one year from date of exercise and two years from date of grant have been met, after which it is considered mature. A disposition of mature ISO stock is a "qualified" disposition.

Maturity Date
Date on which a debt security comes due and must be repaid.

Measurement Date
Under APB 25, the date on which both the number of shares being granted and the price at

which they are granted is first known. For a fixed award, the measurement date is the date of grant; for a variable award, the measurement date can be the vesting date, exercise date, or expiration date. Under FAS 123 and FAS 123R, the measurement date is always the date of grant except in the case of certain performance awards, for which the measurement date is the first date on which there is determined to be a strong likelihood of the performance criteria being met.

Merger
The voluntary combination of two businesses, resulting in one business entity with one stock issued.

Mid-Cap
Refers to either a company or the stock of a company whose market capitalization is between $500 million and $1 billion.

Modification
For tax purposes, any change in the terms of a statutory stock option that provides an additional benefit to the optionee. Modifications of statutory options are viewed as a cancellation of the original option and the grant of a replacement option. The replacement grant must comply with the statutory requirements to retain preferential tax treatment.

For accounting purposes, under APB 25, changes to an award's term that reduce the exercise, increase the number of shares granted, or extend or renew the award. Under FAS 123 or FAS 123R, modifications are simply treated as the granting of new awards for which the incremental difference between the new and old awards must be expensed.

NASD
See "National Association of Securities Dealers."

NASDAQ
National Association of Securities Dealers Automated Quotation System, a computerized system providing brokers and dealers with price quotes by which NASD members trade securities. The NASDAQ Stock Market is an over-the-counter market that competes with the traditional stock exchanges by listing companies' shares for trading, comprised of both the NASDAQ National Market (largest, most active securities) and the NASDAQ SmallCap Market (small emerging growth companies).

The NASDAQ is open for regular trading during market hours, 9:30am to 4pm ET and for after hours trading from 4pm to 6:30pm ET. For holiday and more detailed trading schedules, go to *www.nasdaq.com/about/schedule.stm*. See "Securities Exchange," "Self-Regulatory Organization."

National Association of Securities Dealers (NASD)
Association of securities brokers/dealers that establishes standards and uniform practices for securities trading in the over-the-counter market. Includes all of the major brokerage firms as members. See "NASDAQ."

Net Operating Loss
Tax term describing the state of a company whose business expenses exceed its income in a tax year.

Net Worth
See "Book Value."

New York Stock Exchange (NYSE)
The New York Stock Exchange is the oldest and largest organized U.S. securities exchange. It is regulated by both a fully independent Board of Directors and its advisory Board of Executives composed of member constituents. The purchase and sale of securities on the NYSE trading floor is limited to "members" - firms or individuals who own or lease one of the 1,366 "seats" on the NYSE – who meet directly to transact business.

The NYSE is open for trading during market hours, 9:30am to 4pm ET. For holiday schedules, go to *www.nyse.com/events/NYSECalendarOverviewIndex.html* – Holidays and Hours. See "Self-Regulatory Organization."

No-Action Letter
Publicly accessible letter issued by the SEC in response to a request for clarification of specific securities laws or issues regarding forms. Any protection offered by the interpretation given in the letter extends to only the recipient of the letter, but the clarification provided is generally relied upon as an indication of future treatment of similar issues.

NOL
See "Net Operating Loss."

Nonaffiliate
Any person who is not considered an affiliate under Rule 144.

Noncompete Agreement
Provision in a stock option grant or other compensation agreement that provides penalties, generally the forfeiture of stock or stock options or other specified compensation, if an employee goes to work for a direct competitor within a certain amount of time after termination. See "Clawback."

Non-Derivative Security
Security owned directly or indirectly by a reporting person.

Nonpublic Company
See "Private Company," "Public Company."

Nonqualified Plan
Any stock or equity compensation plan that does not meet the requirements to receive special tax treatment under the Internal Revenue Code.

Nonqualified Stock Option (NQO) (NQSO)
Stock option that does not meet the requirements of a statutory option under Section 422 of the Internal Revenue Code and therefore does not qualify for favorable tax treatment at exercise or disposition. *See Chapter 3: Nonqualified Compensatory Stock Options.*

Nonrecourse Note
Employer-granted loan under which the employer has no recourse to any of the employee's assets beyond the collateral provided. The stock is not considered transferred until the note is fully paid or collateralized. If the note is collateralized solely by the underlying stock, the capital gains holding period begins for tax purposes. Once collateral for the amount of the note in addition to the underlying stock is received, the Rule 144 holding period begins. See "Recourse Note." *See also Chapter 3: Award Purchase Financing: Employer Loans.*

Nonstatutory Stock Option (NSO)
See "Nonqualified Stock Option."

Notice of Exercise
See "Exercise Notice."

NSO
See "Nonstatutory Stock Option."

NYSE
See "New York Stock Exchange."

Offering Date
See "Enrollment Date."

Offering Period
Period during which participants have the right to purchase stock under an ESPP, beginning with the offering/enrollment date and ending on a predetermined exercise/purchase date. *See Chapter 3: Employee Stock Purchase Plan Offering Period Specifics.*

Office of the Law Revision Counsel
Department of the U.S. House of Representatives that prepares and publishes the United States Code, Code 26 of which is the Internal Revenue Code. See "United States Code."

Officer
Any one of a company's principal decision-makers responsible for managing the day-to-day activities of the company. See "Chief Executive Officer," "President," "Section 16 Officer."

Omnibus Pool
An omnibus pool is created when shareholders approve the creation and use of a pool of shares that can be freely allocated by the board of directors among all plans. This can be very useful in a multiple plan situation where the future needs of any one plan are not certain, and are subject to possible rapid change, as in the case of an ESPP. Tracking is relatively simple, as once the pool is in place, all withdrawals are done by board action and simply added to plan pools. See "Pool."

One Million Dollar Cap
See "$1 Million Cap."

Open Window
Period during which employees can freely trade the securities of a corporation. The converse of a blackout period.

Opinion 25
See "APB 25."

Option
See "Stock Option," "Incentive Stock Option," "Nonstatutory Stock Option," "ESPP Option."
See also Chapter 3: Nonqualified Compensatory Stock Options, Chapter 3: Incentive Stock Options.

Option Agreement
Written contract detailing the terms and conditions of a stock option grant.

Option Exchange
A program under which a company offers its employees the opportunity to exchange their underwater options for fewer options at a lower exercise price, according to some formula that sets the exchange ratio to provide essentially the same total value. To avoid variable accounting treatment under APB 25, this program would often be implemented as a "6 + 1" in which participants surrender their old options then wait for at least six months plus one day to receive new grants. This approach is not necessary, however, under FAS 123(R).

Option Exercise
See "Exercise."

Option Exercise Form
Notice of intent to exercise a stock option, the option exercise form is generally completed and submitted to the company along with payment of the total exercise amount for the shares being purchased.

Option Plan
See "Stock Option Plan."

Option Pool
See "Pool."

Option Price
See "Exercise Price."

Option Stock
Stock received upon exercise of a stock option.

Option Term
See "Term."

Option Valuation Model
A mathematical formula designed to assign a value to stock options based on a number of factors related to the option and the underlying stock. See "Binomial Option Pricing Model."

Optionee
An individual or entity who has been granted a stock option.

Options Outstanding
Stock options that have been granted and have not expired or been canceled or exercised. Any plan starts with zero options outstanding. Options granted become options outstanding. Options exercised or canceled cease to be options outstanding. *See Chapter 2: Basic Calculations: Options Outstanding.*

Ordinary Income
Income that is taxed at regular rates, not capital gains.

OTC
See "Over-the-Counter."

Out-of-the-Money Option
See "Underwater."

Outside Director
A member of the board of directors with no familial or business ties to the company or corporation being governed.

Outstanding Grants
Stock options that have been granted but not yet exercised, canceled, or expired. Once exercised, stock options are removed from this calculation.

Outstanding Options
See "Options Outstanding."

Outstanding Shares
See "Shares Outstanding."

Overhang
Granted but unexercised shares. This represents the number of potentially dilutive shares reserved for issuance. One basic formula is (shares outstanding +shares available) / (total shares outstanding). The exact formula differs slightly depending on the firm doing the calculation, but no one standard formula is in widespread use.

Some common formulas include: (1) (options outstanding + options available for grant)/(diluted common shares outstanding [as indicated on 10K]), (2) (options outstanding + options available for grant) / (total shares outstanding + options outstanding + options available), and (3) (outstanding grants + authorized plan shares not yet granted + plan shares pending authorization for current fiscal year)/(total shares outstanding). *See Chapter 2: Basic Calculations: Overhang.*

Over-the-Counter
Method of buying and selling stocks outside of an organized stock exchange, the most prevalent market for which is the NASDAQ.

Overlapping Offering Periods
ESPP offering periods that run concurrently, generally with different offering dates and respectively different purchase prices.

Ownership Guidelines
At companies maintaining ownership requirements, specifications as to how much company stock must be owned by certain executives, directors, or key employees. Generally expressed as a multiple of salary, but occasionally as a specific number of shares.

Par Value
For accounting purposes, a minimal amount that the company must receive for each share of stock that it issues, with no relation to market value. Often expressed as $0.001.

Parachute Payment
Internal Revenue Code term used to describe excessive compensation payments made to executives and key employees that are subject to an excise tax. Parachute payments may be made in cash, stock, or accelerated vesting of large stock option grants. See "Internal Revenue Code, Section 162(m)."

Parent Corporation
A corporation owning a controlling interest in the shares of another company.

Participant
Anyone who has chosen to participate in their company's employee stock purchase plan or other stock plan. See also "Optionee."

Passphrase
EDGAR access code used to create or change a CCC, Password, or PMAC. Not necessary for routine filings, as it is used only to generate a new access code in the absence of the old ones.

Password Modification Authorization Code
See "PMAC."

Pay for Pulse
Term used to describe vesting based solely on the duration of a service period.

PCAOB
See "Public Company Accounting Oversight Board."

Performance-Based Compensation
As defined in IRC Section 162(m)(4)(C), compensation includible in the $1M cap calculation does not include that which is "payable solely on account of the attainment of one or more performance goals" so long as (1) the performance goals are determined by a compensation committee of the board of directors which is comprised solely of two or more outside directors, (2)

any material terms of the remuneration are disclosed to and approved by a majority vote of shareholders before payment, and (3) before payment is made, the compensation committee certifies that all performance goals and any other material terms have been satisfied.

Performance Shares
Stock grants where the number of shares or amount of payment to be received is contingent upon performance goals being met. Performance shares are often not outright stock grants but grants with a value based on the underlying stock where payment is made in either cash or stock. FAS 123 and FAS 123R present no negative accounting treatment for performance shares.

Performance Unit
Grant in which the amount received is measured in a specified dollar value, as opposed to being based on a stock price. Payment and value are dependent upon performance goals being met; payment is made in either cash or stock.

Performance Unit/Tandem Stock Option Plan
A tandem stock option/performance unit plan offers an election at some subsequent date to either exercise a stock option or receive an equivalent amount of stock and/or cash based on the achievement of certain performance criteria.

Generally, at the end of the performance period, the employee may request that the amount earned under the performance unit plan be paid in cash or stock, or the employee may decide to exercise the stock option (whichever the election, the other possibility is canceled).

Tandem fixed stock options usually involve a public company and its subsidiary. The subsidiary adopts a stock option plan in which the employee is simultaneously granted stock options to acquire 1) X subsidiary common shares and 2) X parent shares, where at the date of issuance, both the exercise price and number of shares are known under both grants. No repurchase features are available; the exercise of one cancels the other.

Performance Vesting
Vesting schedule for a compensatory stock award where a specified number of shares is awarded, but vesting is dependent upon performance criteria being met, rather than on the passage of time. To avoid unfavorable accounting treatment under APB 25, most performance options have a cliff vest near or at the end of the option term, with accelerated vesting at each goal achieved. FAS 123 and FAS 123R present no negative accounting treatment for performance vesting.

Phantom Pyramiding
Similar to "pyramiding," an optionee exercises a portion of a stock option, then in theory resubmits the shares received to exercise the option on the remaining shares under the same option, but in fact retains the shares being "submitted," and the company issues a certificate for only the net shares.

Phantom Stock
Phantom stock plans are deferred compensation arrangements based on a theoretical investment in the company's stock. Under a phantom stock plan, employees participate in stock per-

formance but the company avoids issuing options or additional shares of stock in connection with compensation arrangements.

Generally, one phantom stock unit equals the value of one share of stock; at the end of an award period, the employee receives or is credited with a cash amount equal to any appreciation in unit value. During the effective period of an award, the employee generally receives or is credited with dividend equivalents; balances due to the credit of the employee can be paid in lump sums, paid in installments, or further deferred to some future date such as retirement or separation from service.

Physical Delivery
Delivery of an actual stock certificate.

Pink Sheets
Electronic quotation system for trading in OTC securities. The name originally came from the color of the paper that quotation prices were printed on; now they are published by Pink Sheets LLC, a privately owned company not registered with the SEC in any way. Companies whose securities are quoted on the pink sheets do not need to meet any listing requirements and may not be required to file periodic reports or audited financial statements with the SEC. Most are closely held, extremely small, and/or thinly traded.

The Pink Sheets keeps the same holiday schedule as the NASDAQ and is open for trading during regular market hours, 9;30am to 4pm ET. The quotation system is available 7am to 5pm on regular business days.

Plain Vanilla Stock Options
Traditional, basic stock options where the exercise price is equal to the fair market value on the grant date, and vesting is at a measured rate based on length of service with the company.

Plan
See "Stock Option Plan."

Plan Administrator
Person or committee designated by the stock plan as having authority to carry out the actions called for by the plan. Most often the company's board of directors or a subset thereof.

Plan Expiration Date
Date after which awards or grants may no longer be made under the stock plan.

PLR
See "Private Letter Ruling."

PMAC (Password Modification Authorization Code)
EDGAR access code allowing one to change one's password.

Pool
The pool of shares authorized for issuance under a stock option plan but not yet granted. Any stock plan states the number of shares authorized for issuance under the plan. Grants decrease

the number of shares available to issue. Canceled grants are usually returned to the pool to be available again, depending on the terms of the plan. Other shares the plan may allow to be returned include shares exercised but withheld to pay taxes or SARs paid in cash so that the reserved shares are no longer restricted. At any time, the number of shares available for issuance may be increased by shareholder/board approval or due to evergreen provisions. *See Chapter 2: Basic Calculations: Shares Authorized for Issuance (the Pool), Chapter 3: Basic Stock Pool Tracking, Chapter 3: Equity Tracking Spreadsheets.*

Post-Termination Exercise Period
The period of time after an employee's separation from the company during which any outstanding options or other stock awards may be exercised.

Power of Attorney
Legal document assigning the power to manage assets and financial affairs for another person. Can specify which actions can be undertaken and may apply only for a fixed amount of time. May be revoked at any time. Maintained on file at most companies for Section 16 officers to facilitate required filings. See Chapter 4: Section 16 Filings: Power of Attorney.

Pre-Clearance Policy
Company guidelines requiring all transactions in company stock to be approved in-house before taking place. See Chapter 4: Section 16 Filings: Pre-Clearance Policy.

Preferred Broker
See "Captive Broker."

Preferred Stock
Equity securities in a corporation that give priority to holders in regard to dividend payment and distribution of corporate assets upon liquidation.

Premium-Price Options
Stock options granted with an exercise price above fair market value at the time of grant; employees profit from the options only if the share price exceeds the hurdle rate built into the exercise price.

President
Corporate officer subordinate only to the Chairman of the Board. In smaller companies often the same person as the Chief Executive Officer. See "Chief Executive Officer."

Private Company
A company whose shares are not available for public trading. Same as a nonpublic company.

Private Letter Ruling (PLR)
A ruling given by the IRS to a taxpayer in response to a request for interpretation of specific tax laws as they apply to a given set of facts. Any protection offered by the interpretation given in the letter extends only to the recipient of the letter, but a PLR is generally taken as a gauge of what might be acceptable in similar cases. Includes both private letter rulings and technical advice memoranda. See "Internal Revenue Service."

Private Placement
Securities offer that has not been registered with the SEC and involves securities that are bought and sold by parties who negotiate directly.

Privately Held Company
See "Private Company."

Promissory Note
Written agreement between a borrower and a lender documenting the terms and conditions of the credit extended.

Prospectus
Part I of a 1933 Act registration statement. Contains the basic business and financial information on an issuer with respect to a particular securities offering. The prospectus is distributed to interested investors and others who may use it to help appraise the merits of the offering and make educated investment decisions. A prospectus in its preliminary form is frequently called a "red herring" prospectus and is subject to completion or amendment before the registration statement becomes effective, after which a final prospectus is issued and sales can be consummated. See "Securities Act of 1933, Registration Statements."

Proxy
(1) A person designated by a stockholder to vote on his/her behalf, generally to facilitate voting when all shareholders cannot be physically present at a meeting.

(2) The signed document designating such person.

See "Proxy Card," "Proxy Statement."

Proxy Card
When a shareholder vote is required, a shareholder is typically provided with a proxy statement containing information about the matters presented for vote, and a proxy card to authorize designated persons to vote his or her securities on the security holder's behalf in the event the holder does not vote in person at the meeting. See "Proxy," "Proxy Statement."

Proxy Notice
Written notification to shareholders of the time, date, and place of an upcoming corporate meeting, as well as a summary of the matters to be discussed at the meeting.

Proxy Solicitation
Request for authorization to vote on a shareholder's behalf; typically sent by a company to facilitate decision making on routine corporate business matters at the meeting. See "Proxy," "Proxy Card," "Proxy Solicitation Materials," "Proxy Statement."

Proxy Solicitation Materials
State law governs the circumstances under which shareholders are entitled to vote. When a shareholder vote is required and any person solicits proxies with respect to securities registered under Section 12 of the 1934 Act, that person generally is required to furnish a proxy statement containing the information specified by Schedule 14A. The proxy statement is intended to pro-

vide shareholders with the information necessary to enable them to vote in an informed manner on matters intended to be acted upon at security holders' meetings, whether the traditional annual meeting or a special meeting. Typically, a shareholder is also provided with a proxy card to authorize designated persons to vote his or her securities on the security holder's behalf in the event the holder does not vote in person at the meeting. Copies of final proxy statements and proxy cards are filed with the SEC at the time they are sent to security holders. Certain preliminary proxy filings relating to mergers, consolidations, acquisitions, and similar matters are nonpublic upon filing; all other proxy filings are publicly available.

Proxy Statement
When a shareholder vote is required, a shareholder is typically provided with a proxy statement containing information about the matters presented for vote, and a proxy card to authorize designated persons to vote his or her securities on the security holder's behalf in the event the holder does not vote in person at the meeting. The proxy statement is intended to provide shareholders with the information necessary to enable them to vote in an informed manner on matters intended to be acted upon at security holders' meetings, whether the traditional annual meeting or a special meeting. It typically contains biographical and compensation information about the members of the board of directors and the top five company executives, and any proposals for action.

Public Company
A company whose shares are publicly traded. All public companies are subject to the reporting requirements of Section 12 of the 1934 Act.

Public Company Accounting Oversight Board (PCAOB)
A private nonprofit corporation created by the Sarbanes-Oxley Act of 2002, the five member PCAOB reports to the SEC. It registers, inspects, and disciplines public accounting firms, and establishes and enforces auditing standards. Rules established by the PCAOB have the same weight as and are enforced as Rules established under the 1934 Act.

Public Offering
Process whereby a company files for registration under the 1933 Act and offers securities for sale to the investing public. A company's first public sale of securities is known as its initial public offering, after which any number of subsequent offerings may be made, usually for the purpose of raising capital.

Purchase Date
Predetermined date on which ESPP stock is purchased at the end of an offering period. See "Employee Stock Purchase Plan."

Purchase Period
See "Exercise Period," "Employee Stock Purchase Plan."

Purchase Price
Price of one share of stock granted under an employee stock purchase plan. See "Employee Stock Purchase Plan."

Put Option
Derivative security conferring the right to sell a stated number of securities at a fixed price. The converse of a call option.

Pyramiding
Process whereby an optionee exercises a portion of a stock option, then immediately resubmits the shares received to exercise the option on the remaining shares under the same option. *See Chapter 3: Award Purchase Financing: Stock Option Pyramiding.*

Qualified Plan
Any stock or equity compensation plan that meets the requirements to receive special tax treatment under the Internal Revenue Code.

Qualifying Disposition
Disposition of qualified shares (ISO/ESPP) made later than two years from date of grant/enrollment and one year from date of exercise/purchase. Upon a qualifying disposition, the employee typically recognizes capital gains treatment and the company receives no tax deduction. See "Disqualifying Disposition."

Quiet Period
Period before an IPO when company insiders are prohibited from publicly discussing material company information. See "Initial Public Offering."

Rabbi Trust
An irrevocable trust created as a vehicle for tax deferral of ordinary income associated with the exercise of in-the-money NSOs. Assets of a rabbi trust must be available to creditors if other corporate assets are insufficient. *See Chapter 3: Award Purchase Financing: Stock Option Gain Deferral/"Rabbi Trust."*

Readily Ascertainable Fair Market Value
A term describing the value of a stock option that (1) is transferable; (2) is exercisable immediately in full; (3) is not subject to restrictions having a significant effect on the option's value (vesting); and (4) for which the purchase FMV is readily ascertainable. If a stock option has a readily ascertainable fair market value at the date of grant, then the option itself is property transferred as compensation, and the grantee recognizes taxable income equal to the FMV. Most compensatory stock options do not meet one or more of these conditions.

Reconciliation
The process of balancing and updating accounting figures so that they reflect the most current, accurate amounts available. Reconciliations are most often done as of a certain date to give a snapshot of activity at that time, generally at the end of every financial reporting period. *See Chapter 2: Basic Reconciliation.*

Record Date
The date designated by the board of directors as the last date to effect changes in registration of stock before the list of shareholders is set for the next dividend distribution or annual meeting. Only shareholders owning shares as of the record date are eligible to vote at the upcoming meeting or to receive dividends.

Record Owner
The named owner of shares of stock. This may differ from the beneficial owner of the same shares.

Recourse Note
An employer-granted loan that gives the employer recourse to all or substantially all of the employee's substantive assets and under which the employer would intend to enforce that right in the event of default by the employee. Both capital gains and Rule 144 holding periods begin upon receipt of a recourse note. See "Nonrecourse Note." *See also Chapter 3: Award Purchase Financing: Employer Loans.*

Red Herring
Term for a prospectus in its preliminary form. See "Prospectus."

Regional Stock Exchanges
Securities exchanges registered with the SEC and located outside of New York City. See "Securities Exchange."

Registrar
Entity, generally a bank, employed by a corporation to guard against overissuance of the company's stock. Certifies all certificate issuance and cancellation transactions completed by the Transfer Agent. A single entity will often serve as both Registrar and Transfer Agent for a corporation.

Registration
(1) Legal name and address to which a security is registered by the transfer agent; (2) the filing process under the 1933 Act for permission to issue securities.

Registration Statements
(1) Initial two-part registration statement required by the 1933 Act and filed with the SEC before public offerings of securities can be made.

(2) Registration statements required by Section 12 of the 1934 Act and filed with the SEC, kept current by the filing of periodic reports.

See "Securities Act of 1933, Registration Statements," "Securities Exchange Act of 1934, Registration Statements."

Regular Grants
Stock option grants made according to a set schedule and formula, generally on an annual cycle.

Regulation D
"Rules Governing the Limited Offer and Sale of Securities Without Registration Under the Securities Act of 1933," Regulation D provides Rules 501-508 of the 1933 Act. Of these, Rules 504, 505, and 506 provide exemptions to the registration requirements of the 1933 Act. See "Securities Act of 1933, Rule 504," "Securities Act of 1933, Rule 505," "Securities Act of 1933, Rule 506."

Regulation FD
Fair Disclosure rule, requiring public disclosure of any material information communicated to analysts or other market professionals. Intentional disclosures must be simultaneously publicly broadcast; unintentional disclosures must be publicly broadcast within 24 hours or by the start of the next trading day.

Regulation T
Title 12, Chapter II, Part 220 of the US Code, Federal Reserve Regulation T governs the credit extended by brokers and dealers to their clients in connection with securities financing.

Reload Option
A "reload" feature can be added to a stock option grant, where additional options intended to replace optioned shares tendered are automatically issued to an employee who tenders previously owned shares in a stock-for-stock exercise. The new option is granted for the same number of shares and same terms as the shares tendered, but with a new exercise price equal to the FMV at the new date of grant.

One nice feature of reloads is that they provide for continuing stock option grants to key employees, while minimizing dilution because each new grant simply replaces already outstanding stock. Reload options are subject to the same tax, accounting, and securities rules as any other stock option grant.

Reporting Person
For Section 16 purposes, any officer, director, or principal shareholder of a publicly owned company and members of that person's immediate family.

See Chapter 4: Section 16 Filings: Reporting Persons.

Repricing
Under a repricing, companies may invite employees to exchange underwater or poorly priced options for new options priced as of a repricing date set by the board of directors. Generally, repriced options should include new conditions to ensure sufficient consideration to counter shareholder challenges of corporate waste, such as blackout periods, vesting schedule set-backs, or a ratio of new options to exchanged options that is less than 1:1.

When implementing a repricing, be sure to confirm that you conform to applicable provisions of state law and governing plan documents. The decision must also be made to amend existing options or to cancel existing options and grant new options. Will vesting schedules and expiration dates remain intact or be updated as well? What will the new exercise price be? Will the repricing be followed by a blackout period of any length? Schedule execution for a period when you will have adequate time to deal with the increased workload if possible—fiscal year-end is not an optimal time to deal with this additional situation!

Repricing an ISO constitutes a modification of the options for tax purposes. Underwater options are generally not an issue because the modified options are repriced to current FMV, but if the employee declines the repricing, the old option is considered to have been modified by the ability to exercise at a lower price. This can be avoided by issuing offerees an "invitation to receive an offer" that requires them to request in writing an offer to exchange old options for new repriced options. In addition, repricing ISO shares restarts their ISO holding periods and can also affect the $100,000 limitation.

Under APB 25, stock options that are repriced are thereafter treated as though granted under a variable plan for accounting purposes. Under FAS 123R, as under FAS 123, however, repricings are considered new grants, where the original grants have been canceled. Canceling the options does not reverse the compensation expense, so for all unvested options, compensation expense continues to be recorded, but the compensation expense of the replacement grants is no more than the incremental difference between the fair value of the original and the replacement grants.

Repricing of options held by named executive officers can also trigger securities laws requirements, including extensive additional 10-year reporting and potential triggering of short-swing profits recovery under Section 16 of the Exchange Act (the repricing is considered a disposition of old options and acquisition of new ones). In addition, the company may face increased obligations under Rule 13 of the Exchange Act to provide a valid tender offer by filing Schedule TO-1 with the SEC and fulfilling all other tender offer requirements or in accordance with the registration requirements of Section 5 of the Securities Act if the terms of the repriced options are considered to be less advantageous than those of the original options.

Repurchase
A company's reacquisition of shares of stock from a person who acquired the shares through a grant or award from the company.

Repurchase Right
A company's contractual right to buy back unvested stock from a grant or award recipient, most often as the result of termination.

Restricted Securities
Stock that (1) has not been registered under the 1933 Act, or (2) is owned by a control person or affiliate, and must be resold under Rule 144 or another exemption.

Restricted Stock
Under a restricted stock plan, shares are either awarded at no cost or purchased (sometimes at a discount), but ownership is not transferred until vesting restrictions lapse. Restricted stock awards produce less equity dilution than stock options; a 1:3 equivalency ratio would be common, but the exact ratio depends on the stock price, volatility, and other factors.

Vesting is most often time-based, but can be performance-based or tied to company-specific goals. Tax consequences are realized as shares vest, based on the value at the date of vesting unless an 83(b) election is made. Since tax consequences are deferred until the actual issuance of shares, this is a form of deferred compensation, but standard restricted stock is not subject to the deferred compensation provisions of the American Jobs Creation Act of 2004.

See Chapter 3: Restricted Stock Shares.

Restricted Stock Award
Restricted stock awarded at no cost to the recipient. See "Restricted Stock."

Restricted Stock Performance Plans
Plans in which stock is issued upon payment by employee, but ownership does not transfer until performance criteria have been met.

Restricted Stock Shares (RSS)
See "Restricted Stock."

Restricted Stock Units (RSU)
Restricted stock units are restricted stock awards in which the stock is not awarded until after vesting requirements have been satisfied. The future date of issuance is generally fixed at the time the RSUs are granted, typically upon termination of service or after a fixed number of years. 83(b) elections are not available for RSUs. Since tax consequences are deferred until the actual issuance of shares, this is a form of deferred compensation; RSUs are subject to the deferred compensation provisions of the American Jobs Creation Act of 2004.

See Chapter 3: Restricted Stock Units.

Restrictive Legend
See "Legend."

Revenue Ruling
Ruling stating the IRS audit position on interpretation of specific tax laws in regard to a given set of facts. Establishes precedent that others may rely upon.

Reverse Stock Split
A change in capitalization of a company that decreases the number of shares outstanding, and increases the corresponding value of each share. Often undertaken to either raise the price per share to maintain a minimum trading value or to eliminate small holdings to reduce the number of shareholders of record.

Reverse Vesting
See "Early Exercise."

Right of First Refusal
A restriction typically imposed on stock issued by privately held companies. This restriction requires the stockholder to allow the company to match the terms and conditions of any reasonable offers to buy the held stock before accepting the offer.

Right of Repurchase
See "Repurchase Right."

Risk-Free Interest Rate
One of the six variables used in calculating the fair value of a stock option. To calculate, take the average risk-free interest rates for Treasury bonds with the same term as the expected option life, that were issued during the current quarter. If there are no Treasury bonds with terms equal to the expected option term, take the average of the two Treasury bond terms that most closely approximate the expected option term. For interest rates, go to

www.federalreserve.gov/releases and choose: Interest Rates - Daily - Historical Data - U.S. Treasury constant maturities - term = expected option term. See "Black-Scholes Option Pricing Model."

Rule 10b5-1
Rule promulgated by the SEC (under the 1934 Act) that prohibits insiders from trading in securities on the basis of material nonpublic information. Defines the purchase or sale of a security "on the basis of" material nonpublic information to mean that the person making the purchase or sale was aware of the material nonpublic information when the person made the purchase or sale; provides for the affirmative defense against insider trading by establishing guidelines for a written plan for trading securities at predetermined intervals.

Rule 10b5-1 Plan
See "10b5-1 Plan."

Rule 16(b)
See "Securities Exchange Act of 1934, Section 16," "Short Swing Profits."

Rule 17Ad-17
See "Securities Exchange Act of 1934, Rule 17Ad-17."

Rule 144
See "Securities Act of 1933, Rule 144"

Rule 504
See "Securities Act of 1933, Regulation D"

Rule 505
See "Securities Act of 1933, Regulation D"

Rule 506
See "Securities Act of 1933, Regulation D"

Rule 701
See "Securities Act of 1933, Rule 701"

Run Rate
See "Burn Rate."

S-1
See "Form S-1"

S-2
See "Form S-2"

S-3
See "Form S-3"

S-8
See "Form S-8"

SAB 107
Issued by the Securities and Exchange Commission staff, Staff Accounting Bulletin 107 provides guidance to help with the implementation of FAS 123R. *See Chapter 2: Accounting Overview: SAB 107.*

Safe Harbor
A term that describes the range of values that will be accepted as following regulation when no specific value has been stated or required. For example, in making a good faith estimate of fair market value for a private company, "safe harbor" has been granted for the average of two or more independent valuations made by qualified professionals.

Same-Day Sale (SDS)
The exercise of an option for stock in a public company where the cost of the exercise is funded through the sale of the stock acquired under the option. Proceeds are also used to pay tax withholding. *See Chapter 3: Award Purchase Financing: Same-Day Sale.*

Sarbanes-Oxley Act of 2002 (SOX)
Signed into law on July 30, 2002, Sarbanes-Oxley provides sweeping redesign of federal securities laws. Creates the Public Company Accounting Oversight Board to provide accounting and auditing oversight. Requires additional disclosures to and certification as to the accuracy and completeness of financial reports; prohibits personal loans to executives; shortens Form 4 filing deadline; significantly expands financial and penal consequences for securities violations.

Sarbanes-Oxley Act of 2002, Sections 101-103
Establishes and empowers the five member Public Company Accounting Oversight Board to register, monitor, inspect, and discipline public accounting firms and to establish and enforce auditing standards. Provides that Rules established by the PCAOB have the same weight as and are enforced as Rules established under the 1934 Act.

Sarbanes-Oxley Act of 2002, Section 201
Prohibits public accounting firms from providing non-audit services to issuers contemporaneously with an audit, with the exception of certain services provided with the pre-approval of the issuer's audit committee.

Sarbanes-Oxley Act of 2002, Section 302
Requires the CEO and CFO of each issuer to personally certify in statements accompanying the audit report to the completeness, accuracy, appropriateness, and fair disclosure of the financial reports, as well as to the nature and effectiveness of the internal controls supporting the quality of information provided in such reports every quarter. Violation of this section must be knowing and intentional to create liability.

Sarbanes-Oxley Act of 2002, Section 304
Provides for CEO and CFO forfeiture of certain compensation and bonuses in the event of any material noncompliance with financial reporting in relation to misconduct resulting in a restatement of financial statements.

Sarbanes-Oxley Act of 2002, Section 306
Prohibits insider trading during pension fund black-out periods; provides for recovery of profits by the company or shareholders.

Sarbanes-Oxley Act of 2002, Section 307
Requires attorneys representing issuers before the SEC to report evidence of any material violation of securities law or breach of fiduciary duty by a company or its agent to first the chief legal counsel or CEO of the company, then if no response is made, to the board of directors or a committee thereof.

Sarbanes-Oxley Act of 2002, Section 401(a)
Requires additional disclosures in all periodic financial reports of all material off-balance sheet transactions and other relationships with "unconsolidated entities" that may have a material current or future effect on the financial condition of the issuer. Instructs the SEC to issue rules providing for presentation of pro forma financial information in a manner that is not misleading.

Sarbanes-Oxley Act of 2002, Section 402(a)
Prohibits personal loans to executives. Makes it unlawful for an issuer to extend credit to any director or executive officer with the exception of consumer credit companies extending consumer credit in the ordinary course of business to its directors and executive officers on the same terms and conditions offered to the general public.

Sarbanes-Oxley Act of 2002, Section 403
Shortens Form 4 filing deadline. Transactions required to be reported on Form 4 under Section 16 of the 1934 Act must be reported by the end of the second business day (previously the tenth day) following the day of the transaction

Sarbanes-Oxley Act of 2002, Section 404
Requires management to report annually on the internal controls and procedures for financial reporting, including an attestation to the accuracy of that report by the company's auditors.

Sarbanes-Oxley Act of 2002, Section 406
Requires issuers to disclose in periodic reports the existence or lack thereof as well as immediate disclosure of any change in or waiver of a code of ethics for its senior financial officers.

Sarbanes-Oxley Act of 2002, Section 409
Requires issuers to disclose any material information about the company's financial condition or operations in a "rapid and current basis."

Sarbanes-Oxley Act of 2002, Section 802
Makes it a felony to knowingly destroy, alter, or falsify documents with the intent to impede, obstruct, or influence any existing or contemplated federal investigation. Requires auditors to maintain all audit or work papers for five years.

Sarbanes-Oxley Act of 2002, Section 806
Provides whistle-blower protections.

Sarbanes-Oxley Act of 2002, Section 807
Provides for fines and up to 25 years imprisonment for knowingly executing or attempting to execute any type of securities fraud.

Sarbanes-Oxley Act of 2002, Section 906
Similar to Section 302, requires the CEO and CFO of each issuer to personally certify to compliance with Sections 13(a) and 15(d) of the Exchange Act and the material accuracy of the company's financial position and operational results in the company's periodic financial reports.

SAS 70
Statement on Auditing Standards No. 70, "Reports on the Processing of Transactions by Service Organizations," established by the American Institute of Certified Public Accountants in 1993. Provides for outsourcing-service providers to undergo one of two types of annual audits assessing internal controls, and issue attestation reports to outside parties or clients.

For Type I, the organization describes its controls at a certain point in time, and the auditor expresses an opinion on whether the description fairly presented all material and relevant aspects of the controls and on whether the controls were suitable to the desired control objectives.

Type II covers everything in the Type I audit, but also includes detailed testing of the organization's controls over a minimum six month period plus the auditor's opinion on whether the controls tested operated with sufficient effectiveness to provide reasonable assurance that the control objectives were achieved over the testing period. See "Service Auditor's Report."

Schedule TO
Statement of Tender Offer under Section 14(d)(1) or 13(e)(1) of the 1934 Act. Must be filed with the SEC by parties owning five percent or more of a class of the company's securities after making a tender offer for securities registered under the Exchange Act. See "Tender Offer."

SDS
See "Same-Day Sale."

SEC
See "Securities and Exchange Commission."

Secondary Market
Where securities are bought and sold by investors after an IPO.

Secondary Offering
Securities offering that follows an IPO, where holders of previously issued stock sell those shares in a registered public offering.

Section 16
See "Securities Exchange Act of 1934, Section 16."

Section 16 Filings
Every Section 16 insider must file with the SEC a statement of ownership of equity securities issued by the company, and disclose any subsequent stock transactions. Forms 3, 4, and 5 con-

tain information on the reporting person's relationship to the company and on purchases and sales of relevant equity securities. *See Chapter 4: Section 16 Filings.*

Section 16 Insider
A person meeting the criteria listed in Section 16(a) of the 1934 Act: any person who is directly or indirectly the beneficial owner of more than 10% of any class of any registered, non-exempt equity security, or who is a director or officer of the company. Generally refers to any individual holding policy-making authority within the corporate organization, including the president, principal financial officer, principal accounting officer, and any vice president in charge of a principal business unit, division, or function. *See Chapter 4: Section 16 Filings: Reporting Persons, Chapter 4: Section 16 Officer – Initial Information Capture, Chapter 4: Section 16 Officer – Stock Holdings.*

Section 16 Officer
See "Section 16 Insider."

Section 83
See "Internal Revenue Code, Section 83."

Section 83(b)
See "Internal Revenue Code, Section 83(b)."

Section 83(b) Election
Filing under Section 83(b) of the Internal Revenue Code allowing tax liability to be taken at the time of exchange of property (grant of restricted stock, early exercise of stock options, etc.), instead of as restrictions lapse. Filing must be made within 30 days of the date of transfer of property. In the case of equity awards, this means that the tax burden will be calculated at the time of receipt/exercise rather than as the stock vests. If a disqualifying disposition of ISO stock is made, the election applies only to the AMT, not to the ordinary income earned from exercise date to vest date. Once taxes are paid, they will not be refunded or credited for any reason.

Section 162(m)
See "Internal Revenue Code, Section 162(m)."

Section 409A
See "Internal Revenue Code, Section 409A."

Section 421
See "Internal Revenue Code, Section 421."

Section 422
See "Internal Revenue Code, Section 422."

Section 423
See "Internal Revenue Code, Section 423."

Section 423 Plan
See Chapter 3: Qualified Employee Stock Purchase Plans.

Section 424
See "Internal Revenue Code, Section 424."

Section 6039
See "Internal Revenue Code, Section 6039."

Security
Tradable financial instrument evidencing ownership of money or other property.

Securities Act of 1933 (1933 Act)
After the stock market crash of 1929, the 1933 Act was enacted to provide federal regulation of the sale of securities. The 1933 Act seeks to protect investors by requiring issuers to make available financial and other significant information concerning securities being offered for public sale and by making deceit, misrepresentation, and other fraud in the sale of securities illegal. Securities sold in the U.S. must be either registered under the 1933 Act or sold in reliance on a permissible exemption, which registration or exemption applies only to the securities being sold or issued in that offering.

Securities Act of 1933, Registration Statements
One of the major purposes of the federal securities laws is to require companies making public offerings of securities to disclose material business and financial information in order that investors may make informed investment decisions. The 1933 Act requires issuers to file registration statements with the SEC, setting forth such information, before offering their securities to the public. The registration statement, commonly Forms S-1, S-2, S-3, or S-8, is divided into two parts. Part I is the Prospectus, Part II is the information not required to be in the prospectus, which includes information concerning the company's expenses of issuance and distribution, indemnification of directors and officers, and recent sales of unregistered securities as well as undertakings and copies of material contracts.

Securities Act of 1933, Rule 144
"Persons Deemed Not to Be Engaged in a Distribution and Therefore Not Underwriters." Permits the public sale of ordinary transactions in limited amounts of securities owned by affilitates or nonaffiliates holding restricted stock.
- 144(a): any shares of stock issued on the exercise of stock options in reliance upon a nonpublic offering exemption or Rule 506 are "restricted securities" under Rule 144.
- 144(c): requires that the issuer must provide current public information according to the reporting requirements of the Exchange Act or as specified for non reporting companies.
- 144(d): establishes a holding period of one year before sale of Rule 144-restricted stock; loans with nonrecourse notes do not start the Rule 144 holding period.
- 144(e): the aggregate securities sold in reliance upon Rule 144 by any one entity during any three month period may not exceed the greater of 1% of the issuer's shares outstanding or the average weekly reported volume of trading on national securities exchanges during the four week period preceding the filing of Form 144.
- 144(f/g): mandates and regulates the sale of Rule 144 stock only by a registered broker.
- 144(h): if the aggregate securities sold under Rule 144 during any period of three months exceed 500 shares or $10,000, Form 144 must be filed.
- 144(i): Form 144 may only be filed by persons actually intending to sell the stock.

- 144(k): permits unrestricted sale by nonaffiliates of Rule 144-restricted stock that has been held for two years.

Securities Act of 1933, Rule 504
"Exemption for Limited Offers and Sales of Securities Not Exceeding $1,000,000." Part of Regulation D, Rule 504 provides exemption from registration under the 1933 Act for offers and sales by certain issuers meeting specified conditions. The aggregate offering price for an offering of securities under Rule 504 must not exceed $1 million.

Securities Act of 1933, Rule 505
"Exemption for Limited Offers and Sales of Securities Not Exceeding $5,000,000." Part of Regulation D, Rule 505 provides exemption from registration under the 1933 Act for offers and sales by certain issuers meeting specified conditions. The aggregate offering price for an offering of securities under Rule 505 must not exceed $5 million. The issuer must reasonably believe that there are no more than 35 purchasers in the offering, excluding purchasers sharing beneficial ownership and accredited investors.

Securities Act of 1933, Rule 506
"Exemption for Limited Offers and Sales Without Regard to Dollar Amount of Offering." Part of Regulation D, Rule 506 provides exemption from registration under the 1933 Act for offers and sales by issuers meeting specified conditions. The issuer must reasonably believe that there are no more than 35 purchasers in the offering, excluding purchasers sharing beneficial ownership and accredited investors. Purchasers who are not accredited investors must possess a certain level of knowledge and experience in financial and business matters.

Securities Act of 1933, Rule 701
"Exemption for Offers and Sales of Securities Pursuant to Certain Compensatory Benefit Plans and Contracts Relating to Compensation." Provides exemption from registration under the 1933 Act for securities issued for compensatory purposes.
- 701(b): (1) non-investment company private issuers may use this exemption; (2) if a company goes public after offers to sell have been made or grants have been issued but unexercised, that stock may still be issued under this exemption.
- 701(c): exempts compensatory grants to current and former employees, directors, officers, consultants, advisors, and their family members receiving securities as gifts or legal transfers.
- 701(d): aggregate sales in any 12-month period must not exceed the greatest of (1) $1 million; (2) 15% of the issuer's total assets as of the date of its most recent balance sheet or fiscal year-end; (3) 15% of the outstanding securities of the class being offered and sold under Rule 701 as of the date of its most recent balance sheet or fiscal year-end.
- 701(e): if aggregate sales in any 12-month period exceed $5 million, additional disclosure documents must be delivered to investors.
- 701(g): securities issued under Rule 701 are Rule 144 restricted securities but without the Rule 144 one-year holding period and so may be resold under Rule 144 90 days after IPO by nonaffiliates without additional restriction and by affiliates in compliance with the remaining conditions of Rule 144.
-

Securities Act of 1933, Section 3(a)(11)
Exempts securities offered and sold only to persons resident within a single state if the issuer is a corporation incorporated by and doing business within that state.

Securities Act of 1933, Section 5
"Prohibitions Relating to Interstate Commerce and the Mails." Prohibits the sale or delivery after sale of unregistered securities.

Securities and Exchange Commission (SEC)
Government agency established in 1934, charged with supervision and regulation of the securities industry, promoting stability in the markets, and protection of investors. Headquartered in Washington, DC, the SEC consists of five presidentially appointed commissioners, four divisions, and 18 offices, with 11 regional and district offices throughout the country.

The commissioners serve five-year staggered terms ending on June 5 of each year, and no more than three commissioners may belong to one political party. The four divisions are the Division of Corporation Finance, overseeing corporate disclosure of important information to the investing public; the Division of Market Regulation, which establishes and maintains standards for securities market; the Division of Investment Management, which oversees and manages the investment management industry and administers securities laws affecting investment companies and investment advisors; and the Division of Enforcement, which investigates possible violations of securities laws, recommends actions, and negotiates settlements on behalf of the SEC.

Securities Exchange
Organized forum for the buying and selling of securities. Standards are established, maintained, and regulated by the Securities and Exchange Commission Division of Market Regulation. There are currently nine securities exchanges registered with the SEC as national securities exchanges: American Stock Exchange, Boston Stock Exchange, Chicago Board Options Exchange, Chicago Stock Exchange, International Securities Exchange, National Stock Exchange (formerly the Cincinnati Stock Exchange), New York Stock Exchange, Pacific Exchange, and Philadelphia Stock Exchange. See "Self-Regulatory Organization."

Securities Exchange Act of 1934 (1934 Act)
The 1934 Act extended federal regulation to trading in issued and outstanding securities and established and empowered the Securities and Exchange Commission (SEC) to regulate securities activity in the U.S. Under the 1934 Act, issuers are required to file periodic registration statements providing continuous disclosure of financial and other significant information about securities being offered for public sale; self-regulatory organizations, transfer agents, clearance agencies, and broker-dealers are registered and regulated; and insider trading is prohibited.

Securities Exchange Act of 1934, Registration Statements
All companies whose securities are registered on a national securities exchange, and, in general, other companies whose total assets exceed $10,000,000 with a class of equity securities held by 500 or more persons, must register such securities under Section 12 of the 1934 Act. Any company registered under Section 12 of the 1934 Act is obligated to establish a public file containing material financial and business information on the company for use by investors and others, and also creates an obligation on the part of the company to keep such public information current by filing periodic reports on Forms 10-Q and 10-K, and on current event Form 8-K, as ap-

plicable. If registration under the 1934 Act is not required, any issuer who conducts a public offering of securities must file reports for the year in which it conducts the offering (and in subsequent years if the securities are held by more than 300 holders).

Securities Exchange Act of 1934, Rule 17Ad-17
"Transfer Agents' Obligation to Search for Lost Securityholders." Requires every transfer agent to search their databases for any client providing the name or taxpayer identification number of a "lost securityholder." See "Escheatment."

Securities Exchange Act of 1934, Section 10
"Manipulative and Deceptive Devices." Makes it unlawful to use mails or facilities of interstate commerce to do essentially anything the SEC prohibits.

Securities Exchange Act of 1934, Section 12
"Registration Requirements for Securities." Requires any issuer with a class of securities traded on a national securities exchange to register with the SEC, establishing a public file for use by investors and others, then updating the information periodically on Forms 10-Q, 10-K, and 8-K. Empowers the SEC to revoke or suspend the registration of a security if it finds that the issuer has violated any provision of the 1934 Act or its rules and regulations.

Also allows the SEC to (a) summarily suspend trading in any security for a period of not more than 10 days; (b) with the U.S. President's approval, suspend all trading in all securities for a period of not more than 90 days; or (c) in event of a "major market disturbance" take any action determined to be necessary in the public interest and for the protection of investors.

See "Securities Act of 1933, Registration Statements," "Securities Exchange Act of 1934, Registration Statements."

Securities Exchange Act of 1934, Section 13
"Periodical and Other Reports." Requires every issuer with securities registered under Section 12 to file periodic and other reports with the SEC: (a) annual report on Form 10-K, (b) quarterly report on Form 10-Q, (c) current report on Form 8-K for any month in which certain specified events occur.

Securities Exchange Act of 1934, Section 14
"Proxies." Regulates solicitation of proxies from shareholders.

Securities Exchange Act of 1934, Section 16
"Directors, Officers, and Principal Stockholders." Section 16 establishes a reporting requirement and places limitations on certain trading activity in company stock for any person considered a Section 16 insider or officer; a director or officer of the company or the direct or indirect beneficial owner of more than 10% of any class of any registered, non-exempt equity security.
- 16(a): requires Section 16 officers to file Forms 3, 4, and 5.
- 16(b): allows recovery of profits from insiders due to short-swing (purchases and sales within a period of less than six months) transactions.
- 16(c): prohibits short sales and certain similar transactions by insiders.

See "Section 16 Filings," "Section 16 Insider," "Short-Swing Profits." *See also Chapter 4.*

Securities Exchange Act of 1934, Section 18
"Liability for Misleading Statements." Allows any person responsible for a false or misleading statement in any report or filing under the 1934 Act to be held liable in damages by any person who buys or sells securities as a result of the false or misleading statement.

Self-Regulatory Organization (SRO)
SROs are member organizations, including securities exchanges and NASD, that create and enforce rules for their members based on the federal securities laws. See "NASDAQ," "Securities Exchange."

Sell-to-Cover
Stock option exercise transacted through a brokerage firm, where just enough of the exercised shares are sold as necessary to cover the cost (price and tax withholding) of the exercise. The remaining unsold shares are deposited into the employee's brokerage account. *See Chapter 3: Award Purchase Financing: Same-Day Sale / Sell-to-Cover.*

SERP
See "Supplemental Executive Retirement Plan."

Service Auditor's Report
The formal report, including the auditor's opinion, issued at the conclusion of a SAS 70 audit. There are two types of Service Auditor's Reports: Type I and Type II.

The Type I report describes the organization's description of controls at a certain point in time, and the auditor expresses an opinion on whether the description fairly presented all material and relevant aspects of the controls and on whether the controls were suitable to the desired control objectives.

The Type II report covers everything in the Type I report, but also includes detailed testing of the organization's controls over a minimum six month period plus the auditor's opinion on whether the controls tested operated with sufficient effectiveness to provide reasonable assurance that the control objectives were achieved over the testing period.

See "SAS 70."

Settlement Date
The date on which the seller of securities receives proceeds from the transaction and the buyer receives the shares. Brokers are obligated to complete securities trades by the third business day after the trade date, known as "T+3."

SFAS 123
See "FAS 123."

SFAS 123R
See "FAS 123R."

SFAS 128
See "FAS 128."

SFAS 148
See "FAS 148."

Share
One unit of a class of equity securities representing basic ownership interest in a corporation.

Share Certificate
See "Certificate," "DWAC."

Share Price
See "Stock Price."

Share Reserve
Stock that has been authorized and reserved for issuance on exercise of stock options.

Shareholder
Any person who owns one or more outstanding shares of a company's stock, thus receiving voting and other rights. Also called "stockholder."

Shareholder Approval
Authorization of a corporate action by at least a specified percentage of the shareholders of a corporation. Usually has to do with adoption of or changes to stock plans.

Shareholder of Record
A third party, usually a broker or the DTC, who is acting as nominee for a stock's beneficial owner. Shares are said to be held in "street name." This allows beneficial owners to deposit stock certificates as a safekeeping measure, and also to keep ownership holdings confidential from the company.

Shareholder Proposal
Proposal submitted by a shareholder of a corporation for consideration for inclusion on the agenda of the upcoming annual meeting.

Shareholder Value
The perceived or actual value of owning and holding a company's stock.

Shareholders' Equity
See "Book Value."

Shares Authorized but Unissued
Shares of securities of a given class that have been authorized for issuance under a corporation's charter documents, less the number of shares that have been issued. (Shares that have been issued and repurchased are generally not considered authorized but issued, thus you subtract all issued shares, not just issued and outstanding shares, from the authorized shares to determine the number of authorized but unissued shares.) See "Options Outstanding," "Pool." *See also Chapter 2: Basic Calculations: Shares Authorized but Unissued.*

Shares Authorized for Issuance Under the Plan
See "Pool." *See also Chapter 2: Basic Calculations: Shares Authorized for Issuance Under the Plan.*

Shares Exercisable
Option shares available for exercise. Often used to mean vested and available for exercise.

Shares Exercised
The number of shares of stock received upon exercise of a stock option.

Shares Granted but Unexercised
See "Overhang." *See also Chapter 2: Basic Calculations: Shares Granted but Unissued (Overhang).*

Shares Outstanding
The number of shares of company stock currently held by shareholders. Any company, have it one plan or eight, has a specified number of shares authorized for issuance, beginning with the number of shares issued in the initial public offering (IPO). Options exercised for stock, SARs exercised for shares, restricted shares, ESPP shares, and subsequent offerings all increase the number of shares outstanding. Shares repurchased and/or canceled by the company decrease the number of shares outstanding. *See Chapter 2: Basic Calculations: Shares Outstanding.*

Short-Swing Profits
Any profits realized by a company insider from any combination of purchases and sales of the company's equity securities within a period of less than six months. Under Section 16(b) of the 1934 Act, such profits must be returned to the company according to the formula described therein. See "Securities Exchange Act of 1934, Section 16."

Short-Swing Transactions
Any combination of purchases and sales of the company's equity securities within a period of less than six months.

SIC Code
Standard Industrial Classification Code. Used on EDGAR filings to indicate the company's type of business. Also used by the Division of Corporation Finance to assign review responsibility for the company's filings.

Six-and-One
See "6+1."

Small-Cap
Refers to either a company or the stock of a company whose market capitalization is less than $500 million.

Special Grants
Stock option grants made outside of a set schedule and formula, generally one-time grants made for varying purposes.

Spread
(1) The difference between the stock option exercise price and the fair market value of the underlying stock at the time of exercise; or (2) the difference between the bid and asked prices for an over-the-counter stock.

SRO
See "Self-Regulatory Organization."

Staff Accounting Bulletin
Issued by the Securities and Exchange Commission staff, Staff Accounting Bulletins (SABs) present the staff's views regarding accounting-related disclosure practices.

Staff Accounting Bulletin 107
See "SAB 107."

Stapled Options
Spin-off provision through which one stapled option is issued for each share under existing option grant, entitling the holder to one share of the continuing entity and one share of the spun-off entity for each continuing equity share currently held. Stapled options must be exercised simultaneously.

Statutory Stock Option
Any option meeting the requirements of and receiving special tax treatment under Internal Revenue Code Sections 421-424. See "Incentive Stock Option," "Section 423 Plan."

Statement of Financial Accounting Standards
See "FAS," "Financial Accounting Standards Board."

Statement on Auditing Standards No. 70
See "SAS 70."

Stock
Share of capital held by an investor in an organization.

Stock Administration
The handling of issues related to equity distribution by an issuer. *See Chapter 1: How it Works, Chapter 1: The Job Itself.*

Stock Administrator
Person with primary responsibility for managing equity compensation functions in an organization. See "Certified Equity Professional." *See also Chapter 1: Who Are You?, Chapter 1: Where You Fit In.*

Stock Appreciation Right (SAR)
An SAR entitles its holder to a payment of either stock or cash that equals the amount by which shares of stock have appreciated in market value from a specified starting level to the date of exercise.

An SAR is not itself treated as "property" (so a grant is not taxed as a transfer of property) but as an unfunded and unsecured promise to pay either money or property in the form of stock, which in itself is not a taxable event. Once the SAR is exercised and settled, the method of payment determines the tax and accounting treatment.

SARs settled in stock constitute the receipt of gross income in the amount of the FMV (on exercise date) of stock received, and set the holder's basis in the stock received.

The IRS considers SARs exercisable for cash to be deferred compensation, which is taxed to the employee under IRC 61(a); any cash received is included in the recipient's gross income for the year.

Currently, SARs granted pursuant to a program in effect on or before October 3, 2004 where the exercise price is not less than the FMV of the underlying stock on the grant date, and the SAR contains no deferral features, are not subject to the deferred compensation provisions of the American Jobs Creation Act of 2004. In addition, SARs with fixed payment dates may not be subject to the deferred compensation provisions of the American Jobs Creation Act of 2004.

See "Additive SAR," "Freestanding SAR," "Tandem SAR," "Stock-Settled SAR." *See also Chapter 3: Stock Appreciation Rights.*

Stock Award
The grant of vested shares of stock. See "Restricted Stock," "Restricted Stock Units."

Stock Certificate
See "Certificate."

Stock Exchange
Organized market for the buying and selling of stocks and bonds. See "Securities Exchange."

Stock Option
The right to buy or sell a specified number of shares in a corporation at a given price for a specified amount of time. See "Incentive Stock Option," "Nonstatutory Option."

Stock Option Agreement
See "Option Agreement."

Stock Option Plan
Written document describing the terms and conditions under which stock options may be granted to eligible participants.

Stock Option Pool
See "Pool."

Stock Plan
Written document describing the terms and conditions under which equity awards may be made to eligible participants.

Stock Plan Administrator
See "Stock Administrator."

Stock Power
Document evidencing transfer of ownership of a registered security from the record owner to another party.

Stock Price
The price per share of a company's stock, generally determined by market fluctuation.

Stock-Settled SAR (SSAR)
SARs authorizing payment in only shares of stock are economically similar to NSOs, but eliminate the cost of the exercise price. As they are less dilutive than NSOs, SSARs can provide a worthwhile alternative to cashless exercises.

SSARs where the exercise price may never be less than the FMV of the underlying stock on the date of grant, the stock is traded on an established securities market, and the SSARs contain no deferral features other than that related to the exercise price, are not subject to the deferred compensation provisions of the American Jobs Creation Act of 2004.

See "Stock Appreciation Right." *See also Chapter 3: Stock Appreciation Rights.*

Stock Split
A change in capitalization of a company that increases the number of shares outstanding, decreasing the corresponding value of each share. This is generally an effort to reduce the value per share so that it falls within some target range to maximize investor appeal.

Stock Swap
Previously held stock is submitted at current FMV to exercise a stock option. *See Chapter 3: Award Purchase Financing: Stock Swap.*

Stock Symbol
The symbol used to identify a traded security. Symbols with up to three letters are used to identify stocks listed and traded on exchanges; symbols with four letters are used to identify NASDAQ and OTC stocks; symbols with five letters are used to identify NASDAQNASDAQ and OTC stocks other than single-issue common stock; symbols with five letters ending in "X" are used to identify mutual funds. Also called ticker symbol or trading symbol.

Stock Withholding
Withholding taxes due on exercise of a stock option that are calculated and paid in shares of the stock received rather than in cash.

Stockbroker
See "Broker."

Stockholder
See "Shareholder."

Stockholder Approval
See "Shareholder Approval."

Stockholder of Record
See "Shareholder of Record."

Stockholder Proposal
See "Shareholder Proposal."

Street Name
Securities held by a brokerage firm on a client's behalf are registered in "street name," with the shareholder of record being the brokerage firm handling the shares on behalf of the beneficial owner. The client/owner does not receive a physical stock certificate, but does receive an account statement on at least a quarterly or annual basis showing holdings.

Strike Price
See "Exercise Price."

Subsidiary
A company that is majority owned or wholly owned by another company, called the "parent company."

Substantial Risk of Forfeiture
Tax term that applies to compensation whose full transfer is dependent upon future performance of services or upon a goal being met.

Substantially Vested
Tax term that applies to property that is either transferable or is not subject to a substantial risk of forfeiture.

Supplemental Executive Retirement Plan (SERP)
Executive retirement plan used to provide supplemental pension payouts for high-level executives beyond the IRS limits for qualified pension plans.

T+3
See "Settlement Date."

Tandem SAR
Stock appreciation right granted in tandem with a stock option (either ISO or NSO) to facilitate the exercise of an option with no cash outlay. The exercise of either the SAR or the stock option cancels the other. See "Stock Appreciation Right." *See also Chapter 3: Stock Appreciation Rights.*

TARSAP
See "Time-Accelerated Restricted Stock Award Plans."

Tax Deduction
See "Deduction."

Tax Preference Items
Tax deductions available under the regular income tax calculation that are added back to income in the alternative minimum tax calculation. The exercise of an incentive stock option is a tax preference item triggering the AMT calculation.

Tax Withholding
Money a company retains from an employee's or contractor's income for the payment of income and employment taxes.

Taxable Income
Total income less deductions and exemptions.

Tender Offer
Offer made by a company or third party to purchase at a fixed price, usually higher than the current market price, a substantial percentage of a company's shares for a limited period of time, contingent upon the participating shareholders tendering a fixed number of their shares in exchange. Under the Exchange Act, parties owning five percent or more of a class of the company's securities after making a tender offer for securities registered under the Exchange Act must file a Schedule TO with the SEC. In addition, Schedule 13D must be filed by any person acquiring more than five percent of a company's securities directly or by tender offer.

Tender Offer Rule
Rule 13e-4 of the Exchange Act. Regulates tender offers.

Term
The period of time at the end of which a stock option expires.

Termination
(1) Separation of a service provider from the recipient of services; or (2) loss of stock options, either through forfeiture or expiration.

Ticker Symbol
See "Stock Symbol."

Time-Accelerated Options
Stock options with possible acceleration of earliest exercise date or vesting based on performance criteria, similar to time-accelerated restrict stock award plans (TARSAPs).

Time-Accelerated Restricted Stock Award Plans (TARSAPs)
Restricted stock plans with performance incentives. Performance criteria attached to restricted stock affect the timing of lapse of restriction but not the total ultimate award.

Time-Averaged Options
Stock option grants made as a series of grants in smaller amounts spread over a period of time, with the exercise price of each grant the fair market value at each grant date. An alternative to making one large grant at one exercise price.

Time Value
The value received from the ability to hold unexercised stock options for a given period of time; the longer the period of time, the greater the value. This refers to not only the time over which the option removes the risk of owning stock while conferring all the intrinsic value benefits of holding the stock, but to the value of the virtual interest-free loan of the money not tied up in stock ownership.

Trading Symbol
See "Stock Symbol."

Trading Window
See "Open Window."

Tranche
A block of stock options within a larger grant. Often used to describe the blocks vesting at each of a number of vesting dates.

Transaction Codes
Codes used on Forms 3, 4, and 5 to indicate the nature of the transaction being reported.

Transaction Date
Date on which a transaction effecting a change in beneficial ownership occurs.

Transfer
Legal change in ownership of an asset from one party to another, duly recorded in all relevant places.

Transfer Agent
Entity responsible for maintaining the official register of shareholder names, and for effecting registration and transfers of stock. Most private or small public companies have either an in-house person or their corporate counsel act as their transfer agent.

Transferable Stock Option
Stock options that provide by their terms that they may be transferred by the optionee to an approved recipient. Incentive stock options by definition may not be transferable, except upon death.

Transparency
Having financial statements or business processes that are clearly understandable, with no hidden meanings or agendas. Often used in the context of presenting company information to shareholders.

Treasury Stock
Shares of company stock that have been returned to the company, most often because of repurchase or forfeiture. Treasury stock is generally available for regrant or reissue, but its status as "issued" or "outstanding" depends on applicable state corporate law.

Treasury Stock Method
Six step process for calculation of diluted EPS. (1) Assume all option awards/rights are exercised; (2) calculate hypothetical proceeds received by company; (3) include amount paid by employees, average unrecognized deferred compensation, and any tax benefits that would be credited to paid-in capital on exercise; (4) assume hypothetical proceeds used to buy back shares on the open market at the average stock price for the relevant period; (5) if options/awards were issued during the relevant period, average the market price from issuance to the end of period; (6) (number of shares issued) – (assumed shares repurchased) = (net additional shares considered outstanding in diluted EPS calculation).

Trigger
Any event causing a change to the standard terms of a stock or stock option grant.

Trinomial Option Pricing Model
Mathematical formula used to determine the value of a stock option by computing a lattice, or tree, of possible outcomes. A trinomial model assumes three possible outcomes from any point in the lattice, and can be compared to a binomial model in which every other period is skipped, resulting in increased speed and the possibility of more refinement of outcomes, but requiring different variable input parameters than the binomial model.

Underlying Stock
The stock that is reserved for issuance upon exercise of a stock option. See also "Underlying Security."

Underlying Security
(1) The stock that is reserved for issuance upon exercise of a stock option; or (2) the security reserved for issuance upon redemption of a convertible security.

Underwater
Term used to describe stock options with an exercise price higher than the current fair market value. Exercise would cost more than the underlying stock is worth, rendering the options valueless at that point in time. The converse of in-the-money options.

Underwriter
Investment banking firm that facilitates an IPO by buying the shares to be offered from the company, then reselling them to the public at a slightly higher price.

Uniformed Services Employment and Reemployment Act of 1994
Prohibits workplace discrimination and denial of employment benefits on the basis of military service. Allows extended leaves of absence from work for military training or service with the right to reemployment guaranteed by statute.

United States Code
Codification of the general and permanent laws of the United States. Published by the Office of the Law Revision Counsel, it is currently divided into 50 titles by broad subject matter, Title 26 of which is the Internal Revenue Code.

Unrestricted Stock
Stock with no restrictions on resale.

Unvested
Stock or stock options that have not yet vested.

U.S. Code
See "United States Code."

USERRA
See "Uniformed Services Employment and Reemployment Rights Act of 1994."

Variable Accounting
Variable plan accounting. See "Variable Plan."

Variable Award
Under APB 25, an equity award under which either the number of shares being granted or the price at which they will be exercised is not known at the date of grant. See "Fixed Award."

Variable Plan
Under APB 25, stock plan under which either the number of shares being issued or their exercise price is not known on the grant date, resulting in the compensation expense being remeasured at each reporting date until it becomes fixed, varying based on changes to the underlying stock price. Because of the potential volatility of variable plans, variable plan accounting is generally considered less favorable accounting than that for fixed plans. "See Fixed Plan."

Vested
Stock option or stock award in whole or part for which any restrictions placed upon its transfer of ownership have lapsed.

Vesting
Process whereby a stock option or stock award issued with restrictions becomes restriction-free. The presence of vesting restrictions can make an equity award subject to "substantial risk of forfeiture."

Vesting Period
Period over which restrictions placed on a stock option or stock award are lifted.

Vesting Schedule
Sets forth the rate at which the restrictions placed upon stock options are lifted.

Voluntary Filing
The filing of a Form 4 for a transaction that is not required to be reported on Form 4.

W-2
See "Form W-2."

Warrant
Legal document providing authorization for the purchase of a specified number of shares in a corporation at some later date at a given price.

Wash sale
Purchase of stock within 30 days before or after the sale of "identical" stock at a loss, negating the loss realized on the sale.

Window
See "Open Window."

Worthless Stock
Stock in a company that is either completely or effectively out of business and there is no reasonable expectation that the stock might be saleable.

Bibliography

Books

Baker, Alisa. *The Stock Options Book.* 6th ed. Oakland, CA: NCEO, 2004 (2005 supplement available).

Carberry, Ed., ed. *Communicating Stock Options.* 2nd ed. Oakland, CA: NCEO, 2002.

Hamilton, Robert W. *The Law of Corporations.* St. Paul, MN: West Group, 2000.

Kraus, Herbert. *Executive Stock Options and Stock Appreciation Rights.* New York, NY: Law Journal Seminars-Press, 1994, updated annually.

Nadel, Alan A., Thomas M. Haines, and Gregory M. Kopp. *Accounting for Equity Compensation.* 2nd ed. Oakland, CA: NCEO, 2004.

Ratner, David L. *Securities Regulation.* St. Paul, MN: West Group, 1998.

Rodrick, Scott S., ed. *Selected Issues in Equity Compensation.* 2nd ed. Oakland, CA: NCEO, 2005.

Rosen, Corey, et al. *Beyond Stock Options.* 3rd ed. Oakland, CA: NCEO, 2005.

———. *Equity Compensation in a Post-Expensing World.* Oakland, CA: NCEO, 2003.

Tax and Securities Sources for Equity Compensation. 2nd ed. Oakland, CA: NCEO, 2005.

Thomas, Kaye. *Consider Your Options: Get the Most from Your Equity Compensation.* 2005 ed. Lisle, IL: Fairmark Press Inc., 2005.

Articles

Austin, Linda. "Options Trade Checklist." www.naspp.com (2001).

Baksa, Barbara. "Understanding FASB's New Standard on Equity Compensation" www.naspp.com (2005).

E*TRADE Business Solutions Group, Inc. "Faster Than the Speed of Light: Section 16 Reporting Under Sarbanes-Oxley" (downloaded white paper). www.etrade.com (2003).

Flores, Jazzlyn. "Equity Year-End Checklist." www.naspp.com (2003).

Needham, Karen. "FAS 123 Footnote Questionnaire." www.naspp.com (2004).

Vitale, Denise. "Stock Plan Audit and Control Checklist." www.naspp.com (2004).

Vitale, Denise. "Plan Administration: Data Matters-Financial Reporting." www.naspp.com (2003).

———. "Director and Officer Questionnaire." www.naspp.com (2004).

———. "FAS 123 Black-Scholes Valuation Checklist." www.naspp.com (2004).

———. "Glossary of Stock Plan Terms." www.naspp.com (2004).

———. "Year-End Checklist." www.naspp.com (2004).

———. "Year-End Tax Checklist." www.naspp.com (2004).

Periodicals

CEP ¢ents (CEPI)
Employee Ownership Report (NCEO)
The Stock Plan Advisor (NASPP)

Web Sites

cepi.scu.edu (Certified Equity Professional Institute)
uscode.house.gov (Office of the Law Revision Counsel, United States Code)
www.amex.com (American Stock Exchange)
www.beysterinstitute.org (Beyster Institute)
www.fairmark.com (Fairmark Press)
www.fasb.org (Financial Accounting Standards Board)
www.fwcook.com (Frederic W. Cook & Co.)
www.gpoaccess.gov/uscode/ (Government Printing Office, United States Code)
www.iasb.org (International Accounting Standards Board)
www.irs.ustreas.gov (Internal Revenue Service)
www.issproxy.com (Institutional Shareholder Services)
www.law.uc.edu/CCL (Securities Lawyer's Deskbook, University of Cincinnati College of Law)
www.mystockoptions.com (myStockOptions.com)
www.naspp.com (National Association of Stock Plan Professionals)
www.nasd.com (National Association of Stock Dealers)
www.nasdaq.com (NASDAQ)
www.nceo.org (National Center for Employee Ownership)
www.nyse.com (New York Stock Exchange)
www.perkinscoie.com (Perkins Coie LLP)
www.pinksheets.com (Pink Sheets)
www.sec.gov (Securities and Exchange Commission)
www.sia.com (Securities Industry Association)
www.ustreas.gov (U.S. Department of the Treasury)

Conferences

NASPP Annual Conference (various sessions)
NCEO Annual Conference (various sessions)
CEP Institute Annual CEP Symposium (various sessions)

About the Author

Amy Yamashiro's working life includes growing up in a family-owned jewelry store, leading a marketing organization, and heading the membership department of a member-based international nonprofit civil rights organization. She began working in stock plan administration in 1997, and was excited to be a key member of a highly successful IPO team in early 2000. Amy currently provides independent consulting services in stock plan administration and can be reached at amy.yamashiro@gmail.com.

A member of the National Association of Stock Plan Professionals, the National Center for Employee Ownership, and the CEP Institute Society, Amy received her BA from Wellesley College and is a Certified Equity Professional in good standing.

About the NCEO and Its Publications

The National Center for Employee Ownership (NCEO) is widely considered to be "the single best source of information on employee ownership anywhere in the world" (*Inc.* magazine, August 2000). Established in 1981 as a nonprofit information, research, and membership organization, it now has thousands of members, including companies, professionals, unions, government officials, academics, and interested individuals. It is funded entirely through the work it does.

The NCEO's mission is to provide the most objective, reliable information possible about employee ownership at the most affordable price possible. The NCEO publishes a variety of materials on employee ownership plans, creating an ownership culture, and the research on employee ownership. The NCEO offers online training programs on both ESOPs and equity compensation plans. In addition, the NCEO holds dozens of live meetings, conferences, and Webinars on employee ownership annually. The NCEO's work includes extensive contacts with the media. Finally, the NCEO has written or edited six books for outside publishers.

Membership Benefits. NCEO members receive the following benefits:

- The bimonthly newsletter *Employee Ownership Report*, which covers ESOPs, stock options, and employee participation.

- Access to the members-only area of the NCEO Web site, including the NCEO's referral service, a searchable database of well over 200 service providers; a searchable ESOP lenders directory; a searchable archive of past and present NCEO newsletters; a glossary of ESOP and equity compensation terms; status updates on legislative and regulatory matters; case studies; a discussion forum; and more.

- Substantial discounts on publications and events produced by the NCEO (such as this book).

- The right to telephone or e-mail the NCEO for answers to general or specific questions regarding employee ownership.

How to Join. An introductory NCEO membership is $80 for one year. For service providers, membership covers a single person (unless you join as a Referral Service member, in which case other people at your office are included). Otherwise, membership covers your company. To join, see the order form at the end of this book, go to our Web site at *www.nceo.org*, or call us at (510) 208-1300 with your credit card in hand.

Selected NCEO Publications

The NCEO offers a variety of publications on all aspects of employee ownership and participation, from employee stock ownership plans (ESOPs) to stock options to employee participation. Below are descriptions of some of our main publications.

We publish new books and revise old ones on a yearly basis. To obtain the most current information on what we have available, visit our Web site at *www.nceo.org* or call us at 510-208-1300.

Equity Compensation Plans

- This book, *The Stock Administration Book,* is a comprehensive guide to administering stock options and other equity compensation plans.

    $50 for NCEO members
    $75 for nonmembers

- *The Stock Options Book* covers the legal, accounting, regulatory, and design issues involved with stock options and stock purchase plans.

    $25 for NCEO members
    $35 for nonmembers

- *Selected Issues in Equity Compensation* is more detailed and specialized than *The Stock Options Book,* with chapters on issues such as securities laws and evergreen options.

    $25 for NCEO members
    $35 for nonmembers

- *Accounting for Equity Compensation* is a guide to the financial accounting rules that govern equity compensation programs in the United States.

    $35 for NCEO members
    $50 for nonmembers

- *Beyond Stock Options* is a guide to phantom stock, stock appreciation rights, restricted stock, direct stock purchase plans, and performance awards. A CD with model plans is included.

    $35 for NCEO members
    $50 for nonmembers

- *Equity Compensation in a Post-Expensing World* addresses how to choose and structure equity compensation plans when expensing is required.

    $25 for NCEO members
    $35 for nonmembers

- *Employee Stock Purchase Plans* covers how ESPPs work, tax and legal issues, administration, accounting, and other matters.

    $25 for NCEO members
    $35 for nonmembers

- *Model Equity Compensation Plans* provides stock option and stock purchase plans, in print and on diskette.

    $50 for NCEO members
    $75 for nonmembers

- *Communicating Stock Options* offers practical ideas and information about how to explain stock options to a broad group of employees.

    $35 for NCEO members
    $50 for nonmembers

- *The Employee's Guide to Stock Options* is a guide for the everyday employee.

    $25 for NCEO members and nonmembers

- *Equity-Based Compensation for Multinational Corporations* covers how to extend stock options and other equity-based programs worldwide.

    $25 for NCEO members
    $35 for nonmembers

- *Incentive Compensation and Employee Ownership* is a broad look at how companies can use incentives.

    $25 for NCEO members
    $35 for nonmembers

Employee Stock Ownership Plans (ESOPs)

- *The ESOP Reader* is an overview of the issues involved in establishing and operating an ESOP in a public or private company.

    $25 for NCEO members
    $35 for nonmembers

- *Selling to an ESOP* is a guide for owners, managers, and advisors of closely held businesses. It explains how ESOPs work and covers legal structures, valuation, financing, S corporations, and the tax-deferred Section 1042 "rollover."

    $25 for NCEO members
    $35 for nonmembers

- *Leveraged ESOPs and Employee Buyouts* discusses how ESOPs borrow money to buy out entire companies, purchase shares from a retiring owner, or finance new capital. It is applicable to both public and closely held companies.

    $25 for NCEO members
    $35 for nonmembers

- *The ESOP Communications Sourcebook* provides ideas for and examples of communicating an ESOP to employees and customers. A CD with communications materials is included.

    $35 for NCEO members
    $50 for nonmembers

- *The ESOP Committee Guide* describes the different types of ESOP committees, the goals they can address, alternative structures, member selection criteria, training, committee life cycle concerns, and more.

    $25 for NCEO members
    $35 for nonmembers

- *ESOP Valuation* brings together and updates where needed the best articles on ESOP valuation that we have published in our *Journal of Employee Ownership Law and Finance*.

    $25 for NCEO members
    $35 for nonmembers

- The *Employee Ownership Q&A Disk* gives Microsoft Windows users point-and-click access to 500 questions and answers on all aspects of ESOPs in a fully searchable hypertext format.

    $75 for NCEO members
    $100 for nonmembers

Miscellaneous

- *The Journal of Employee Ownership Law and Finance* is a quarterly journal covering ESOPs, stock options, and related subjects in depth.

    One-year subscription: $75 for NCEO members, $100 for nonmembers

- *Ownership Management* draws on the experience of the NCEO and leading companies to explain how to build a culture of lasting innovation by combining employee ownership with employee involvement programs.

    $25 for NCEO members
    $35 for nonmembers

- *Section 401(k) Plans and Employee Ownership* focuses on how company stock is used in 401(k) plans, both in stand-alone 401(k) plans and combination 401(k)–ESOP plans ("KSOPs").

    $25 for NCEO members
    $35 for nonmembers

Order Form

To order, photocopy this page and fax it (with your credit card information) to 510-272-9510 or mail it (with your credit card information or a check) to NCEO, 1736 Franklin Street, 8th Floor, Oakland, CA 94612; call us at 510-208-1300 and order over the phone using your credit card; or order securely online at *www.nceo.org*. If you are not yet a member but join now, you will pay the lower member prices for any publications you buy at the same time.

Name

Organization

Address

City, State, Zip

Country (if not U.S.)

Telephone   Fax   Email

Payment Method   ❏ Check (payable to "NCEO")   ❏ Visa   ❏ M/C   ❏ AMEX

Credit Card Number

Expiration Date   CVV code (Visa/MC only; last 3 digits in signature area)

Signature

Checks are accepted only for orders from the U.S. and must be in U.S. currency.

Title	Qty.	Price	Total

Subtotal	$
Sales Tax	$
Shipping	$
Membership	$
Total Due	$

Tax: California residents add 8.75% sales tax (on publications only, not membership or subscriptions)

Shipping: In the U.S., first publication $5, each add'l $1; elsewhere, we charge exact shipping costs to your credit card, plus a $10 handling surcharge; no shipping charges for membership or Journal subscriptions

Introductory NCEO Membership: $80 for one year ($90 outside the U.S.)